He's Not Lazy

He's Not Lazy

Empowering Your Son to Believe In Himself

Adam Price, PhD

STERLING
New York

STERLING
New York

An Imprint of Sterling Publishing Co., Inc.
1166 Avenue of the Americas
New York, NY 10036

ISBN 978-1-4549-1687-1

Library of Congress Cataloging-in-Publication Data
Names: Price, Adam, (Psychologist), author.
Title: He's not lazy : empowering your son to believe in himself / Adam Price.
Description: New York City : Sterling Publishing Co., 2017. | Includes
  bibliographical references and index.
Identifiers: LCCN 2016009991 | ISBN 9781454916871 (hardback)
Subjects: LCSH: Teenage boys--Psychology. | Parenting. | Maturation
  (Psychology) | BISAC: FAMILY & RELATIONSHIPS / Life Stages / Adolescence.
  | FAMILY & RELATIONSHIPS / Parenting / General. | PSYCHOLOGY /
  Developmental / Adolescent.
Classification: LCC HQ797 .P75 2017 | DDC 305.235/1--dc23
LC record available at https://lccn.loc.gov/2016009991

Distributed in Canada by Sterling Publishing Co., Inc.
ᶜ/ₒ Canadian Manda Group, 664 Annette Street
Toronto, Ontario, Canada M6S 2C8
Distributed in the United Kingdom by GMC Distribution Services
Castle Place, 166 High Street, Lewes, East Sussex, England BN7 1XU
Distributed in Australia by NewSouth Books
University of New South Wales, Sydney, NSW 2052, Australia

For information about custom editions, special sales, and
premium and corporate purchases, please contact Sterling Special Sales
at 800-805-5489 or specialsales@sterlingpublishing.com.

Manufactured in the United States of America

6 8 10 9 7

sterlingpublishing.com

Contents

To my family: Beth, Jonah, and in loving memory of Sam.

Introduction

———

Recently I bumped into the mother of a young man I treated some years ago, a boy named Kyle. This is a moment of truth for any child psychologist. Usually our patients graduate from therapy and move on to the next stage of their lives; we rarely get to find out whether our efforts had any lasting effect.

When I first met Kyle as a tenth grader, he was floundering in school. Though he didn't exhibit the warning signs of a truly troubled adolescent—drug use, outright rebellion, cutting school, or violent outbursts—he'd grown completely and utterly apathetic in the academic sphere. He was seriously phoning it in, which is why his parents had given him the nickname "Mr. Bare Minimum"— he did just enough to stay above the fault line, getting a D in Spanish and a mix of B's and C's in his other classes. Although he did see friends on weekends, when he was home Kyle spent most of his time in his room, curtains drawn, in front of a computer screen. He was very difficult to rouse in the morning and was often late for school. His parents were so worried that Kyle's lack of motivation would have very real repercussions on his future, they went so far as to have him tested by a psychologist for learning disabilities. The psychologist observed, "Kyle has lost his motivation to succeed at school, and does not do his homework. Instead he prefers to text his friends, listen to music, and play video games. He feels that nothing about school interests him, and has failed several tests that he did not study for." Yet the doctor made no suggestions about how to help Kyle get more motivated. After reading the report I understood why Kyle's parents were so frustrated—his IQ was in the ninety-first percentile.

They, like so many of the parents I see, were overwrought. How could a boy with so much promise risk his future by not even attempting to earn the grades that would get him into a "good" college? Nothing they did seemed to make a difference. Grounding only made Kyle belligerent, but backing off left him to flounder even more.

Kyle was typical of the kind of patients I've come to see more and more of in the practice I maintain in New York City and New Jersey—boys described by teachers and counselors as "good kids," but who very obviously lack the motivation to succeed in middle and high school.

Much has been written about the kinds of pressures kids are under today. But the media coverage tends to focus on the problems of the super-achieving academic elite—kids who are enrolled in multiple Advanced Placement courses and volunteering at the local soup kitchen while mastering an obscure Chinese classical instrument and holding down spots on several sports teams. Though these kids, whose parents take a Harvard-or-bust mentality, *are* under real pressures—as evidenced by the very disturbing rise in the abuse of stimulant drugs as study aids—there is another, typically overlooked class of boys who manifest their stress in different, less obvious ways. These are the boys I worry about—the ones who make time for Netflix®, video games, Snapchat, Facebook, Instagram, and friends, but not for school. Many, like Kyle, do the minimum that's required in order to get by, flying under the radar of official "trouble" while causing their parents plenty of grief and consternation.

Though they look like they're impervious to academic pressures on the outside, their behavior is, in fact, a direct response to the stress they're experiencing. Contrary to appearances, these kids aren't just lazy—they're overcome by demands that they fear they simply cannot meet. And so, in the face of pressures they feel they cannot handle, they choose to "opt out" of the competition altogether. These opt-outs are the subject of this book.

There is no question that our achievement-oriented, competitive culture has created a pressure cooker for today's adolescent. Teenage boys are extremely sensitive to this stress, and as a psychologist I see its victims daily. Bright and capable boys complain of feeling inadequate and ineffective. But rather than working harder and staying up later, they react to this pressure by shunning their work altogether, propping up their fear-based rebellion with justifications like "I am not going to be one of those nerds who have no life," or "Tests don't measure intelligence or help you learn, so what's the point of studying for them?" They protect themselves by turning to avoidance and denial—the primary coping mechanisms of adolescence.

The world through which these boys are navigating is infinitely more complex than that experienced by their parents. Regardless of the quality of their schools, kids these days are being asked to juggle like never before. Over the past twenty years, high school students have added an extra class to their school days, with 7 percent also taking more rigorous courses. As much as technology may enrich the learning experience, it has also created an information overload for students. Teachers email assignments to kids after class and deadlines are pushed to midnight, thanks to Turnitin.com. Gone are the days of handwritten term papers and poster-board presentations. Now students must be able to create flashy

Excel® slide decks, participate in wikis, tweet reading responses to their classmates, and post on class Facebook pages. Their extra-curricular activities are generally plentiful and varied—part of a hyperextended college prep process begun as early as elementary school. Meanwhile, their friends are texting (incessantly) and their online world of choice awaits, buzzing with messages and notifications as soon as the dismissal bell rings, if not throughout the school day.

This increased volume of work, stimuli, and play requires the organizational skill of a business executive. But teenage brains aren't maturing any faster these days. The adolescent brain is a developing entity, with many boys still in the process of obtaining the focus, attention to detail, and planning capabilities that are called for by these increased obligations. There is a growing consensus among psychologists, physicians, and educators that adolescence extends well into a person's twenties, when the brain is fully "matured." So it's no surprise when the obligations go unmet, particularly by boys. Nationwide, there's been a well-documented decline in the number of boys who attend college—with girls more likely not only to be accepted, but also to earn better grades and to graduate. Boys are also much more likely than girls to be diagnosed with learning disabilities and with behavior disorders such as attention deficit hyperactivity disorder (ADHD)—diagnoses I see in many of my patients.

The big-picture problem of boys and learning is not news—to the contrary, it's been the subject of a vast ongoing national discussion, with many education specialists theorizing that boys are at an intrinsic disadvantage in a classroom that discourages their natural tendency to be active and competitive. But where does this leave parents of underperforming teen boys in the here and now?

The day I ran into Kyle's mom, I was relieved to learn that he had made it to and through college after all and was now working in software development; there were even plans for graduate school afoot. Kyle was a perfect example of a kid who needed the pressure dial turned down in order to pull himself up by his own bootstraps. While on the surface, opt-outs do look lazy, dig a little deeper and you will often find a very conflicted boy, one who wants to do well but is afraid to fail, and so does not try. This book will help you suss out these hidden obstacles and help your son face his fears.

There is lots of research about motivation, but very little practical advice that applies to teens. Teens are complicated, so we need to have a comprehensive approach that accounts for all the moving parts. This book is divided into two parts. In part I, I will help you to take a fresh look at your son and to understand all of the radical changes going on inside his body and mind. We will need to get our heads around how boys are different than girls. The way they learn, relate to their friends, seek status, and talk about their feelings: These all have bearing on how we approach boys who opt out. By the end of this section it will be clear to you why your son is not lazy. You will then be ready for part II, which is chock-full of suggestions to get you out of the conflict stage and into the problem-solving stage. I have worked hard to offer meaningful insights, and then turn these into actionable steps you can take.

By now you are probably deep behind enemy lines, in the thick of a major power struggle over your son's grades and the amount of time he spends studying. A negotiated truce will rest upon insight into the way your son embroils you in his tug-of-war. I call this entanglement the Paradoxical Response, and you can read about it in chapter 7. This and future chapters will put you on the right side of your son's passivity and paralysis (his side) and teach you to end power struggles and improve communication. Once the conflict is diminished, we will set to work on the underlying problem—a lack of confidence in his learning abilities and a "fixed mind-set" that allows the teen to believe there's no hope for change because his abilities are etched in stone. From here out we will focus on the key components of motivation, all tailored to the unique demands of adolescence: control, competence, and compassion. You will learn how to talk to your son in a way that puts the responsibility for change in his hands, thus respecting his autonomy. You will also be provided with the tools to help your son gain self-awareness and manage the anxiety that underlies his lack of motivation.

He's Not Lazy will help you understand that your son is not lazy—he is struggling. And this is important, because acceptance is ultimately the best help a parent can offer. You will begin to understand why your son feels he can't do the work on his own (perhaps partly because you are too willing to do it for him). You will see how much of his behavior grows out of a fear of seeming stupid or untalented. You will discover patience and the understanding that perhaps the problem lies not with your son, but rather with the world, for asking so much of a boy who will eventually get there, but needs more time. Ultimately, you will learn to trust him enough to grant him more freedom—the freedom to fail, to learn about himself, and to find his own motivation and drive. For once he does—even if it takes him longer than some of his friends—this motivation will be truly his, and no one will be able to take it away.

But first, let me reintroduce you to your son.

He's Not Lazy

The first part of the book corrects a common but destructive assumption that parents make about their son: He is lazy. This dangerous misconception causes parents to miss the root of their son's problems and, because he feels blamed by them, further alienates him. Chapter 1 encourages parents to see their son in a different frame (paradigm shift). The remaining chapters take a fresh look at the cognitive and emotional transformation that defines adolescence, while detailing the implications these changes have for the teenage boy who is opting out. This section will provide parents with an understanding of their son's psychology and reframe his problem. Understanding how teens view the world and how their minds work is crucial to developing effective strategies to help motivate them.

1

Let Me Reintroduce You to Your Son

Let me reintroduce you to your son. If he is a typical under-achieving teen, he complains bitterly about everything that is wrong with school. The teachers are stupid, the curriculum is irrelevant, math is just moving numbers around, and English is just moving words around. No one ever needs to know geometry, and Shakespeare is an absolute waste of time. Meanwhile you never see him studying. He is the boy who has no homework but his grades are slipping.

Here is what you have probably done so far. When you are not sick with worry, you are nagging. Or maybe you are fighting—with him and/or with your spouse or co-parent. You have been so anxious about his future that you have pestered him constantly about homework and upcoming tests. You may have even enrolled him in a summer science class, as suggested by his college admissions counselor. Maybe you took him to see a therapist. To others he looks like a nice kid, soft-spoken, engaging, and polite, but to you he seems unmotivated, maybe even lazy. All of your begging, pleading, and berating have failed to light the fire of motivation under your son.

If you have picked up this book, chances are the following comments and questions, posed by some of the parents who attend my lectures, will strike a chord:

- "What options do I have left when consequences don't work? I take away his phone, the computer, and he just says, 'Fine, take it away. I don't care.'"
- "I don't know how to talk to my son anymore. When I try, he grunts or says, 'Leave me alone.'"
- "He is only motivated if he likes a teacher, or if he is really interested in the subject. Otherwise, forget it."
- "If only he worked a little harder, if only he cared a little more . . ."

If you want to get to know your child better, take out a ruler. Ask him to rate how important school is for him on a scale from one to twelve. Then ask him to rate his social life and extracurricular activities. You'll be surprised, but he will likely score highest, at least nine or above, on the school question, second on the social question, and last on the extracurricular question. Now use the same ruler to ask him how capable he feels of success in each of these areas. Don't be shocked if the order is reversed. In other words, things are not always what they seem. Your son actually wants to do better in school; he just does not think he is able to. His apparent laziness actually traces back to a fear of failure, otherwise known as anxiety. This type of anxiety is present in all unmotivated, underachieving teens, including those with learning disabilities, those with attention deficit hyperactivity disorder (ADHD), and those who deal with the challenge of adolescence by resorting to substance abuse or promiscuity. Whether your son's low self-esteem is the cause of his school problems or merely secondary to any of the above conditions, it's the first thing you need to address in order to help your son.

But here's the thing. Where most parents fail is thinking that in order to improve their son's self-esteem they have to shower him with praise. The truth is that praising kids with low self-esteem is just as problematic as criticizing them. Deep down your son feels that you are measuring and evaluating his performance, which makes your love appear conditional. So in this case positive feedback is not the way to go any more than is negative feedback. What you have to do is to stop evaluating and measuring him.

And in case you haven't figured it out yet in your own life, you cannot force another person to change. That is particularly true about your teenage son. The tide is definitely against you here. While your son is not an adult, he thinks he is, and he certainly wants to be treated like one. At the very least, he wants to be treated like a free agent, and the only thing standing in the way of this daydream is you. He therefore must fight you off even if the only way he can do that is by getting worse. So what's a parent to do?

In his book *The 7 Habits of Highly Effective People* Stephen Covey describes his experience with his own teenage son, who was failing socially, academically, and athletically. At first he and his wife encouraged him to be positive and hopeful. When this didn't work, they sent him to therapy. But that made him feel that there was something wrong with him, which made the situation even worse. At some point Covey decided that his relationship with his son was more important to him than his son's success. He knew that the key to having a better relationship was to accept him as he was, rather than wishing him to be someone else. As a highly educated man who had made it to the top of his profession, this was impossible to achieve without undergoing what he calls a "paradigm shift." To get there, Covey had to evaluate his entire belief system and the conventional wisdom about success and what is important in life. It was only when he became convinced that success, as defined by our society, was not important to him that he was able to accept his son as he was. As he reports, once he made this "paradigm shift," his son started to improve in school and socially, ultimately turning the corner to become a motivated and successful teen.

Whereas Covey tells us this story to illustrate the meaning of a paradigm shift, for our purposes the import of this story is that the parent stopped focusing on his son and instead started to focus on himself. So rather than evaluate your son's performance, use the following exercise to refocus your attention on yourself.

Write down three to five strengths and weaknesses that describe you as a person. Be honest in writing down your weaknesses; don't treat this like the typical job interview question, where your weakness is really a strength ("I care too much"). Next, as unpleasant as it might seem, zoom in on your weaknesses. Think of examples where they've caused you embarrassment, shame, or humiliation. Recall how you failed because of those weaknesses. Now imagine how much better you would feel about yourself if your kid was a brilliant student and got into an Ivy League school. That would be great, wouldn't it? But is that your son's responsibility, to make you feel better about yourself? And furthermore, is criticizing him about his weaknesses going to correct them? Clearly, it has not worked so far.

So let's try something different: Try to accept that your weaknesses are a part of who you are. You have done your best throughout your life to try to improve, but you are imperfect. Try to forgive yourself and accept yourself for who you are, with these problems. Pause here and take a breath to contemplate this notion. If you can do that, you've already gained more understanding of your son, as well as more distance from his struggles. You can now begin to be more objective about what would help him. It is only when you reach this level of objectivity that you can develop a plan to help your child.

If greater objectivity is the first essential ingredient, greater empathy is the second. To get there, focus on how you felt about yourself as a teenager. Try to recall the cool boy or girl who did not give you the time of day. Remember the teacher who humiliated you in front of the class. Did you ever get a 70 on a math test and not tell your parents about it? What was the worst grade you ever got? What about those parties that you weren't invited to? What about that truly stupid thing you did or said to someone that you still regret?

Once you allow yourself to become immersed in these experiences, you will feel more empathy for your son and will be able to see the world from his point of view. Armed with these two essential ingredients—objectivity and empathy—you are ready to become not just a well-intentioned parent, but also a helpful one.

Now let's do one more thing to really sharpen your ability to empathize and be objective. It's an exercise called "Who do you see when you look at your child?" Take out a piece of a paper and jot down your answers to the following questions:

1. How is your child like you? Not like you? Your spouse/ partner?
2. What do you hope he becomes (not just happy)?
3. What are your regrets about your childhood, your adult life? What mistakes have you made that you hope your son does not?
4. What aspects of life do you wish were easier for your son than they were for you?
5. What childhood experiences were important for you? Do you want your son to have the same ones (going to the same summer camp, college)?

6. Which of his interests are the same as or different from yours?

7. Which interests do you feel good about? Which are his interests that you couldn't dream of sharing in a million years? Which do you feel uncomfortable with or disapprove of? Do you consider any to be a waste of your child's time? If so, why?

8. Is he critical about anything about himself? What does he put himself down about? What are the personal limitations that he struggles with?

9. Write a description of your child. Try to write it as an objective, compassionate observer. Don't refer to him as your son or child. When you are writing this, just refer to him by his name.

The Four Sons

I hope at this point I have dispelled the belief that your son is lazy. He does not lack motivation to do well in school—*he has mixed feelings about trying his hardest.* He is insecure about his chances of academic success, an insecurity that often stems from ambivalence about becoming an adult.

While the issue of self-esteem cuts through the difficulties of all teenagers, there are several distinct types of kids who fall under the opt-out umbrella. For the sake of simplicity we will break it down into four types. There is some overlap, and you may recognize your child in more than one category. These descriptions should give you a clearer picture of why your son opts out.

MR. OPPOSITIONAL

Patrick O'Donnell was extremely polite to adults other than his parents or teachers. Friends' parents, his parents' friends, even I, his therapist, were safe from the antagonism Patrick saved for the authority figures in his life. In therapy, he complained bitterly about everything that was wrong with the prestigious private school he attended. The administration made stupid policies, did not care about the students, and offered a curriculum that was "irrelevant." Tellingly, while he had no time for school assignments, Patrick was a voracious reader. He favored the *New York Times*, books on politics, and websites such as *Politico* and *RealClearPolitics*. But you wouldn't have known it from his report cards.

Patrick's father, whose own hard work and discipline had landed him a partnership at a prestigious New York law firm, frequently battled with Patrick over his grades, study habits, and lack of motivation. Mr. O'Donnell asked to see his son's homework each night, spoke to his son's teachers frequently, and took away Patrick's laptop when he missed assignments. He even tried paying Patrick to do his homework. However, the more restrictions he imposed, the more Patrick shut down and blamed the school and his father for his failure. Patrick was upset about the way a lot of things had been handled during his parents' divorce, things that he had no control over. In some ways, rebelling against school was his revenge—it made his parents angry, and when they were angry he held the reins.

Patrick fits the mold of a type of boy I call Mr. Oppositional. Mr. Oppositional tends to be bright and opinionated. He is a power struggle waiting to happen. He makes teen rebellion into a competitive sport, frequently challenging his parents' authority and sometimes his teachers' as well. His goal is to protect his independence at all costs, often because his parents are too controlling. He is defiant because he is angry. By the time they reach my office, the parents of Mr. Oppositional are worn out. They feel they have lost the battle.

If your son is anything like Patrick, the problem is that you have become the enemy. You probably took too strong a hand in helping him stay on top of his studies when he was younger (maybe because you felt it was the only way he could pass), and now all he wants is to knock you from your throne. You are also too willing to engage in lengthy negotiations with him about the consequences of getting bad grades. You have trained him to be a good lawyer, and to never take no for an answer. He has probably been talking you out of consequences for many years now. These negotiations are power struggles in disguise, and power struggles are the death trap of parenting a teenager. Since the only thing that matters to your teen in this battle is his sense of autonomy or control, he has nothing to lose. He will escalate the conflict as high as he has to in order to win.

MR. DO-IT-FOR-ME

Max's parents were desperate. They wanted someone to convince him to do his homework. Max was failing school and jeopardizing college. However, he was also a local legend. What started as an occasional gig deejaying school dances grew into an entertainment company that competed with professionals on the wedding and bar mitzvah circuit. As an entrepreneur, Max showed real promise. But his deejaying left little time for school. He only did his homework with a tutor, whom his parents had hired to come twice a week. He only ate if meals were served on a tray in his room. ("Otherwise he will not eat," said his mom.) And at sixteen, his mother still picked out his clothes.

The classic Mr. Do-It-for-Me does not pick up his clothes from the floor, do the dishes, or turn in his own homework assignments on his own. There is no need, with his parents hovering close by, ensuring that everything goes well for him. This overindulgence is not about parents giving too much in the material realm; it's about parents doing too much. Therefore, it's not a problem exclusive to affluent families. Mr. Do-It-for-Me's parents mean well—they are often trying to compensate for a problem their son faces, such as ADHD. They make sure he completes his homework by sitting with him, ensure that he makes it to practice on time by packing his soccer bag, and believe they are doing the right thing by dialing down expectations and requiring nothing of him other than passing grades.

As a result, these boys end up believing they are truly special and that things will come easily to them. They come to rely on the tutors, coaches, and therapists their parents hire to assist them, and end up with unrealistic expectations about how far they can go in life with little effort. Mr. Do-It-for-Me needs to change—but so do his parents.

Mr. Popular

Cameron could make waiting for a bus entertaining. He was always upbeat and playful, and he loved to have a good time. He only listened to music that made him feel good, a philosophy that extended to most of his life. His nickname was "the Camster." Most people liked Cam, and though sometimes cocky, he was not the type to put other kids down. He was a star soccer player who always placed his sports and social life above school. That is, until poor grades jeopardized a future college scholarship and caused Cameron to realize that he needed to shift his priorities. Desperate to try anything in order to play soccer in college, Cameron agreed to therapy. And it turned out there was one thing Cameron was not very confident about: his intelligence.

With his back up against the wall, he had no choice but to apply himself. Knowing how competitive Cameron was, I bet a bag of his favorite candy (Cam loved candy) that he could not turn in his homework every day for a month. It was a bet I was eager to lose, and did. I also challenged Cameron's notion that he was born with a fixed amount of brainpower and could not get any smarter (we will talk about this in chapter 12). These things helped, and Cameron turned his grades around.

Life could not be better for Mr. Popular. He is often an exceptional athlete or has tremendous appeal. People admire his natural talents and are drawn to his personal style and charisma. Mr. Popular has gotten used to the instant gratification that his talents bring. The future looks bright—things are going well in high school, so why should the rest of his life be any different? He is sure that his talents will glide him into college, maybe with an athletic scholarship to boot. Meanwhile, deep down, he may doubt his intelligence; so far he has been able to sneak by. You, too, may have fallen prey to his charm or valued his athletic feats above all else. You may also have cut him too much slack for carousing or hanging with his crew, even as he was failing at school.

MR. UNCERTAIN

Unfortunately, the sophistication of Aiden's humor was lost on the average eighth grader. Though he was exceptionally sharp, few people "got him." His parents knew how bright he was, but this only made them angrier that he was not an A student. The well-meaning intentions of a teacher backfired when the career inventory she administered indicated that Aiden should become a landscaper. Somehow this finding proved to Aiden that he just did not measure up. He loved all things technical and took pride in knowing more about computers than anyone in his grade, but his teachers only seemed interested in his lack of effort. He complained that they did not like him. Though he played sports, Aiden did not feel especially good at them. So he took refuge in video games, the one area where he felt competent, and which provided status among his friends.

Even though others recognize him to be bright, Mr. Uncertain often has little confidence in his own abilities and is usually socially insecure as well. He has not yet discovered his strengths and feels helpless, suffering from a lingering sense that he is simply not good enough. He would rather hide behind a lack of effort than take a risk that might prove he is really not so smart after all. Unlike Mr. Oppositional or Mr. Do-It-for-Me, Mr. Uncertain does not express his anger directly at his parents. Rather, he turns it on himself, which sometimes results in depression.

As his parent, you are definitely frustrated by Mr. Uncertain's lack of effort, but you do not always know what is going on with him. He may have a learning issue you do not understand. You may have held him to too high an academic standard without appreciating how insecure he really is.

Myth Busters

Now that you've met a few opt-outs, it's time to really break out of the "He's Just Lazy" paradigm and into a new one. In order to do so, a few myths need to be debunked.

MYTH 1: HE'S UP FOR THE CHALLENGE

Do you believe your son is actually intellectually and emotionally ready to take on all of the challenges thrown his way? He isn't. More boys are opting out because, in the past two decades, the goalposts have been moved: Educational demands have dramatically increased. What used to be a manageable playing field now requires extraordinary drive and talent. A kindergarten teacher recently told me, "Ten years ago we expected the children to be able to count to twenty by the end of the year. Now it is one hundred." Fourth grade used to be the year of the big curriculum bump—when children had to make the leap from learning to read to reading to learn. Fourth grade was also typically the time when learning disabilities started to emerge, and parents would call me to evaluate their child. Now students are expected to make this transition by third grade, which is part of the reason why we, in education and psychology, think there's been an uptick in the number of young children diagnosed with learning disabilities and ADHD. Educators are also concerned about the number of parents who want to "red shirt" their sons—wait a year to enroll them in kindergarten, in order to give them an edge. It used to be that when the demands were reasonable and age-appropriate, kids with minor learning issues could still learn to compensate on their own. This is not the case when even "normal" kids are struggling to keep their heads above water.

Decades ago, boys who lacked motivation were called late bloomers. Today, however, we call them underachievers. A late bloomer has a chance to catch up; an underachiever is already behind. Eventually the late bloomer will find his way, but the underachiever needs help and he needs it now. Helping kids to become more efficient, so that they can deal with unrealistic expectations, is not always going to work. Keep that in mind before you throw more money at the problem by hiring tutors, therapists, and academic coaches. These services might help, but they are not going to "fix" your son.

MYTH 2: HE'S NOT WORKING UP TO HIS POTENTIAL

As a ten-year-old boy I received some shocking news: I was not living up to my potential! At least this was the report delivered to my mother, at the annual parent-teacher conference, by Ms. Beca, my fourth-grade teacher. Although this feedback was meant to prod me to greater academic heights, it only led to confusion. I took this to mean I was not smart enough. Was there some unfulfilled level of accomplishment out there I had yet to reach? Have I achieved it yet? Have you?

The prevailing myth is that opt-outs have "more potential," potential that somehow needs to be unlocked. We fall into the trap hinted at by a recent advertisement for the March of Dimes®, which asserts, "Every baby is born to do something great." As a nation, we've bought in to an obsession with greatness. Americans have always believed that with a little grit and ingenuity, any goal is reachable, any obstacle surmountable. We conquered the frontier and put a man on the moon. However, children cannot be made "new and improved" with each generation. Potential is a wolf in sheep's clothing—it's a term that sounds like it is all about growth, but which has really become synonymous with competition. When parents complain that their son is not achieving his potential, what they are really saying is "I believe he's so smart that if worked up to his potential 100 percent of the time, he'd be at the top of his class." The danger here is that all of the emphasis is placed on the outcome, rather than on the process. Our race to produce top-performing students who have achieved their potential by the age of eighteen may be robbing them of the very thing they need most to succeed: enough space to learn by trial and error, enough freedom to learn on their own, and enough time to grow. Even though this is, seemingly, the biological purpose of adolescence, these days we want to speed up the process.

More damaging, however, is the way this pressure to perform distracts us from core values that children need to learn—the value of owning our work rather than getting a parent or tutors help to polish every paper or project, the value of taking time to do household chores rather than dedicating each effortful hour to homework, and the value of experiencing minor failures and setbacks so that you know how to pick yourself up, dust yourself off, and try again. When it comes to children, we must ask ourselves, "Potential for what?"

MYTH 3: OVERPARENTING WILL HELP YOUR SON

After fifty years of economic growth, it's dawning on parents that their children can no longer count on doing better economically than they have done. Historian Paula Fass asserts that this worry is pushing well-meaning moms and dads to do more than just prepare their kids for the future: They are trying to take full control of it. With enough oversight, tutoring, and coaching, they misguidedly believe they can commandeer their children's natural course of development and compensate for any genetic shortfalls that might make them less competitive. Instead of accepting our sons' limitations and giving them the space to grow, we become overinvolved and controlling to make sure they stay at the head of the pack. If the trend continues, parents will be using drones instead of helicopters to monitor their children. As we shall see, all of this help may have actually contributed to your son's opting out. What's more, instead of preparing your son for the future, all this frantic preparation may be robbing him of it.

What I have learned, in over twenty years as a clinical psychologist, is that, above all else, these kids need less pressure and more time to develop. Yet this is not what most parents feel free to give them. Most parents aggravate the problem by either getting overly involved or not setting firm enough limits. Many do both at the same time—they oversee and they nag, but they never hold their sons accountable for the choices they make.

It is naive to think that boys can be pushed to excel through sheer force of parental oversight. In fact, overparenting may be responsible for having created the problem in the first place. Those "helicopter parents" we hear so much about, the parents whose chief offense is the loving impulse to do too much for their kids and to pay too much attention, may in truth actually be diminishing their children's chances of developing their own wellsprings of motivation and productivity.

By the end of this book you will have shifted paradigms to one where your son is not lazy. Instead, you will realize that his brain is still developing; he is searching for manhood, worried about his future, and in need of greater autonomy, more accountability, and the freedom to fail. You will learn to ask different questions, listen more closely to his answers, and give him the trust he needs, so he can begin to believe in himself.

Before moving on I will leave you with this. Mark Kelly is head of the lower school at the Assumption School in Houston, Texas. He has years of experience in education, having taught in Boston and New Orleans before landing in Houston. Mark told me that parents frequently approach him to say, "I have done everything I can possibly think of for my son, but he is still struggling. What more can I possibly do." To this pleading Kelly bluntly replies, "You have done everything but step out of the way."

2

Shifting Bodies, Shifting Minds

Picture yourself walking through your neighborhood. Everything looks just the same today as it did yesterday. Same buildings, same street posts, and the same crack in the sidewalk that you often trip over when you don't watch out: "Samesville, USA." There's a sense of security in the familiarity. Now imagine taking that same stroll, but this time things are slightly off kilter. At first you can't put your finger on exactly what has changed; it's just a feeling. Then you realize that all of the buildings have shrunk—maybe an inch or two—just enough to weird you out. The next time you take a stroll, there's an even a bigger change. The dry cleaner and the pharmacy have switched sides of the street. This is what it feels like to go through puberty. A teen's world seems to be shifting before his very eyes and everything—himself, his friends, even you—looks different.

It is no wonder then, that your son's moods and behavior are unpredictable. One second he is mature and sophisticated and then, moments later, it's as though you have a two-year-old. What you see on the outside is how he feels on the inside. Sometimes your teen *is* that sophisticate who holds opinions about world politics, and other times he is not. He'll even regress and have tantrums.

Teens, by nature, are inconsistent. For the first time, they are beginning to develop true empathy, the ability to put themselves in someone else's shoes. Yet they are simultaneously some of the most self-centered people on the planet. Their intellectual abilities take off; an adolescent can grasp abstract concepts such as "democracy" and "justice." It's also, however, a time when impulsivity, poor judgment, and bad choices are typically at full tilt. How, you may wonder, can any human be such a delight and then, seemingly instantaneously, evoke a depth of rage you never thought possible? One day you think, *This kid is going to take the world by storm*, and the next you worry that he might not actually graduate from high school. Don't worry—you are not alone.

Teens go through a physical, intellectual, and emotional metamorphosis. Watching your son navigate puberty is simultaneously fantastic and frightening. It's a joy to see him mature, expand his awareness, and become more independent. The changes, however, come on so rapidly that it can be unsettling for everyone involved. Not only are there the physical changes to contend with, but on a deeper level your son is grappling with profound questions—questions that just a few years ago would have made no sense to him but that, in a few years more, must be answered if he is to make the transition from dependent child to self-reliant adult: *Who am I? What do I believe in? What should I become, and do I have what it takes to get there?* Although these questions might always linger to some extent, right now they are in the forefront of your teen's mind. They impact his day-to-day decision making. An important part of adolescent development, this self-inquiry is both exciting and overwhelming.

The answers to these questions for your son are found in a variety of unexpected places: when he's hanging out with friends, reading *Lord of the Flies* (which he swears is boring), or even searching for a new look at the mall. Every time a teenager engages in school, in an extracurricular activity, or in risk taking, he discovers something new about himself.

However, some teens find this process of self-discovery too confusing. While they take unwarranted risks at the skate park, in school they fear that a failure or even a less-than-perfect outcome will expose their (perceived) inadequacy. This is one of the main reasons that teens opt out. Think of development like a river, and your son is stuck in an eddy. For clarification, and the sake of this analogy, an eddy is a little whirlpool formed by obstacles that spins around aimlessly. In order to help your opt-out, we need to find out where these obstacles are hiding. Your son is not lazy. Chances are that the biggest contributors to his eddy-like condition are things over which he has no control.

This chapter will examine the most significant of these obstacles: the pace of his physical, cognitive, and emotional development.

From Childhood to Adolescence

To understand what teenagers are growing into, we have to appreciate what they are leaving behind. Dr. Marsha Levy-Warren explains this in very simple terms: "Children feel small in a world that is divided between the big and the small, and feel safe knowing that those who are big care for those who are small." Kids see the world through their parents' eyes. They know who they are because they know who they belong to—which team to root for, which religion to believe in, who to be just like when they grow up. Mom and Dad rule because they are king and queen.

Being small and feeling that their parents care about them gives children an important sense of continuity. After the first year of life, growth is gradual. Your son gets up every morning feeling he is still the same boy he was the day before. As long as there is

peace, he imagines that the reign of Mom and Dad will endure forever. Metaphorically, childhood is like Samesville; structure and
consistency make kids feel safe. Even though an elementary school–
aged boy can fantasize about eventually being an adult, he can't
really imagine a life without the support and care of his parents.
When my son was in fourth grade, he asked me if it was hard to
get a job as a waiter. Where did this question come from? Food
service had never been on his list of "things to be when I grow
up." Apparently, his thinking went like this: "Someday I will go to
college, but after that I will obviously move back home. I'll need a
job because grown-ups have jobs. There is a pizzeria in my town,
and I could probably work there." He even asked if it was okay to
live at home until he saved enough money to buy a house in the
neighborhood. (That nearby house still sounds good to me.) This
seemed like the perfect solution for a boy who knew he would
grow up but could still only see himself as forever nine years old.
To paraphrase Dorothy at the end of *The Wizard of Oz*, *If it's not
in the backyard, I don't need it.*

Little boys do grow and eventually become men. The thing is,
however, for most of our adult lives (just as when we were kids) the
aging process happens in the background; we slip into middle age
and then, one day, realize we are old. Adolescence does not work
that way. It seems to happen all at once. Although puberty actually
lasts a few years, there is nothing like a little pubic hair to tell a
child, "You are not in Kansas anymore." The terrain of Samesville
changes, seemingly overnight. Puberty interrupts a child's sense of
continuity and with it an understanding of who he is in the world.
A feeling of consistency will return once your son feels at home in
his new, bigger self. He won't become a completely different person,
but even you don't know what kind of adult your son is going be. He
has quite a challenge ahead of him. The eleven-year-old only has to
become a twelve-year-old. However, the twenty-one-year-old must

become an independent adult who can get a job, raise a few kids of his own, and perhaps even make the world a better place. The survival of the species depends on it. Moving out into the world is one of life's most challenging transitions; it's decades in the making. There is a lot riding on the shoulders of your teenager.

Ambivalence

In order to be successful, your teen will have to stop depending on you the same way he did when he was younger and learn to rely on himself. As you've probably already realized, this dependency will not go down without a fight. Childhood does not gently give way to adolescence, and you will see this acted out in all manner of ways. As an early teen, at one moment he'll try to bully you into a later curfew, and in the next he'll want to curl up beside you on the couch. Privacy will mean everything until he forgets about it and runs through the house in his underwear. And then there are the socks left all over the house, because secretly your boy still wants to be treated like that little kid who was so well cared for.

However, your son also wants to believe he's outgrown you. After all, that's exactly what he tells his friends. With them he acts big and tough. It's exciting to walk with his friends to the pizza parlor and eventually to drive places by himself. He thinks he's ready to do things that you know he's not ready to do. But at the same time, he still wants your care. Puberty is a river that separates childhood from adulthood. The bridge that crosses that river, that carries your son from dependence to independence, is called ambivalence.

The meaning of *ambivalence* is often misunderstood. Many think it means a lack of strong feelings one way or the other. "I could go to the movies *or* stay home. Either way is fine with me." What it means, though, is that you concurrently have two sets of very intense and often competing feelings: "I really want to go to the movies *and* I really want to stay home." While it is impossible to go and stay at the same time, you can be both excited and scared about something, for instance, a new job. Ambivalence causes us to approach and retreat. Your son really wants to grow up . . . and he really doesn't.

Ambivalence is the essence of adolescence. It will drive you crazy, and it defines almost everything your son does. Some days he will march proudly to "the independence side" of the bridge, and you will feel as proud of him as he feels about himself. Other days he will make a run for the other end. That might be wonderful, if it takes the form of hugs, but not so wonderful if his ambivalence is manifested in a screaming match.

Shifting Bodies

The transition from dependence to independence starts with the physical changes of puberty. For your son, these changes are the first indication that he's losing the continuity he has relied on for so long. He's no longer little, though he is not quite big. And there is no way to mistake him for the child he once was. He is taller, hairier, and has started to smell. During the first two to three years of adolescence, your son's skeleton will increase by 45 percent, and he will accumulate 37 percent of his total bone mass. I have noticed teens grow bigger from one weekly therapy session to the next!

Physical growth during adolescence is a haphazard affair. J. M. Tanner, whose scale became the go-to measure of sexual development, observed that "a boy stops growing out of his trousers a year before he stops growing out of his jacket." Teenage boys are often clumsy because they have yet to figure out how to coordinate limbs that have grown out of proportion to their torso. For a time, a teenage boy may wear a man's shoe size but still shop in the boys' department. Those big feet certainly get in the way. This growth spurt—and the muscles that come with it—will propel some boys forward on the athletic field. For others, who may have been ahead of the curve as children, an advantage is lost. These changes make an adolescent very self-conscious, in part because they are linked to sexual development, but also because they cause uncertainty. In the midst of puberty, a child is never confident he is doing it "right." A seventh grader becomes an eighth grader when all of his friends do, but he may be one of the few boys in his class to have a deeper voice or, perhaps more unsettling, one of the few who does not.

This new body also takes a lot more care; it needs to be deodorized, shaved, and occasionally fumigated. Steps toward independence are taken as your son begins to manage these tasks on his own. Do you still need to remind him to take a shower? Can he get up in the morning on his own? He has to reevaluate himself in light of his increased size and strength. This includes figuring out how to relate to his parents, over whom he suddenly has the advantage of a few inches.

A growth spurt has a psychological impact as well. It creates a very physical barrier between your son and his childhood. He realizes for the first time that a phase of his life is over. The toddler knows he is not a baby, but he does not really recall this happening. The five-year-old knows he can reach the sink and tie his shoes, but he does not think, *My toddler days are behind me.* Not so with an adolescent. It is always funny to hear teens reminisce about being children, as if it were a long time ago. To them, childhood was a very different time. Crossing the threshold into adolescence makes your son aware of something he's never noticed before: the passage of time. This opens up the possibility that life does not last forever—a devastating thought for anyone. Along with this possibility comes the daunting awareness that adulthood is just around the corner, and he'd better get a move on.

There is one more change brought on by puberty—probably the most difficult one for parents to bear. Abruptly, your son does not want to talk to you anymore. He doesn't want you to come into his room, to ask how school was or what his friends are up to. He'd rather stream a movie alone in his room than watch the same movie with you in the family room. A sixteen-year-old patient recently told me, "I have not been into my family lately. I don't really care about them or want to be with them. My dad does not like this too much. That bothers me because I do not want to worry about that."

Up until this point, although he's had his own life, you have always shared in almost every aspect of it. You brought cupcakes to his class, spoke to his teachers, cheered his goals, and applauded his performances. You know his friends; they have probably slept at your house. Now your son wants some distance because he has a secret: He is now a sexual human being, and you are the last person he wants to know about it.

Any awareness of your son's sex life will come strictly by accident. Because he wants to avoid these accidents at all costs, he will shut you out as much as possible. Anthony Wolf, author of *Get Out of My Life, but First Could You Drive Me and Cheryl to the Mall?*, wrote: "Sexuality is extremely important to the teenage male, and since he wants to keep it separate from his parents, he keeps himself separate from his parents." I witnessed a family friend grow up, largely from one Thanksgiving to the next. Somehow puberty scared his smile away. For a time, this once vivacious and friendly boy barely said a word to his family. Rarely would a laugh, or even a giggle, escape his wary mouth. It's as if KEEP OUT, NO TRESPASSING was written all over his face. Fortunately, he's grown into a warm and engaging young man with children of his own. The cold war on parental relations does not last forever. Your son will open up again once he becomes more comfortable with his sexuality. Only then it will be as a young man who is beginning to experience a life of his own.

Shifting Minds

While the physical changes of puberty may create a one-way exit from childhood, it's the quantum leap his thinking takes that will ultimately help him resolve those burning questions of meaning and existence now before him. A teen's thinking skills do not just "unfold" or "blossom"—they explode.

A young child's thinking is anchored in the world of the concrete. He can only apply reason to things he has experienced, touched, or seen. He tries to bring sense to things by making up theories about what he observes, but abstract concepts are beyond a child's reach. He understands the concept of "country" because he lives in one. He knows that America is a democracy because he has seen his parents vote. He may even understand what a monarchy is, having grown up with stories about kings and queens. However, ask a fourth grader what role free speech plays in a democracy and you will be met with a blank stare. A bright eighth-grade patient was complaining about being taunted by a boy in his class who had "problems." I asked if he knew the meaning of the saying "People who live in glass houses shouldn't throw stones." He answered: "If they do, they will hit themselves. They will hit the glass and break it." On his own, my young patient could not yet extract the symbolic meaning of this idiom. However, give him a few months and his mind will make that amazing leap to abstract thought. I still remember being confounded by the notion that "a pound of feathers weighs the same as a pound of bricks." Then one day it just clicked.

Abstract thought is the gateway to conceptual thinking. Unlike a child, a teen does not have to experience something in order to understand it. He can test out the theories he forms in his mind without being dependent on direct experience. These theories help him not only to better understand how things are, but also to imagine how they could be. For example, by using deductive and inductive reasoning he can see relationships between scattered facts, even if some information is missing. With deductive reasoning, one begins with a general principle and then applies that principle to more a more specific case. *All high school juniors have homework. John is a junior. Therefore John has homework.* Inductive reasoning is the opposite. It starts with the pieces and uses them to figure out the general principle. *I saw three kids at the deli during lunch so they must have a day off from school.*

These thinking skills also help teens to do something that might surprise you—appreciate cause and effect. Of course there will be numerous times when he is not thinking about the consequences of his behavior (like when he sneaks out in the middle of the night or drives off with an open bottle of vodka in the car). However, he is now capable of wrapping his head around a history paper about the origins of the American Revolution.

We don't only think in words. Visual-spatial reasoning is an equally important area of development. This type of thinking involves understanding images and space, such as being able to detect visual patterns and analyze spatial relationships. If you have ever put a puzzle together, you have used both visual-deductive reasoning (looking at the picture on the box to figure out where all the pieces go) and visual-inductive reasoning (collecting all the corners, or gathering all the pieces with blue and white to make the sky).

There's more good news! Now your son can think about thinking. This is called metacognition, and it will allow your teenager to evaluate his own thoughts as well as the conclusions of others. A child has only one frame of reference: his own. He's at the center of his universe, not because he is selfish, but rather because it's the only way he *can* look at things. As far as he's concerned, his teacher exists only when he can see her; at the end of the day she hangs herself up in the classroom closet until the next morning. With adolescence, however, comes perspective and the ability to put oneself in another's shoes. This new capacity to see things from another perspective opens the door to empathy and self-awareness. From this newly acquired vantage point, your son is now able to consider how others view him. So, when he questions your logic in grounding him for missing curfew, remember that he's just taking his newfound abstract reasoning skills out for a spin. While you are holding firm to the consequences, appreciate how smart he's getting.

There are now whole new worlds for your son to ponder: politics, art, even spirituality. One of the reasons I love working with teenagers is because they are so passionate about all of their new ideas. They are capable of intellectual conversation. Do not worry too much about the conclusions your son may draw in this new stage of development. Critical thinking has just begun for him. Ask your son's opinion on world events or the book he's reading in English class. He may even have something interesting to say about his favorite video game.

A New Sense of Right and Wrong

The capacity for abstract thought allows your son to make progress in another sphere: moral reasoning. The sense of right and wrong develops along with the child. For little kids, morals are a matter of cause and effect; young kids follow the rules to avoid punishment. Gradually children develop an inner moral sense. In the beginning, they strive to be "good" children, friends, or classmates, in order to win the approval of others. The next step, which *usually* emerges in late-elementary- and middle-school-aged children, is an understanding that the whole community benefits if everyone follows the rules.

The pinnacle of moral development is a very abstract idea: "the social contract." This contract is based on the concept of "the common good"—that every community member must sacrifice some personal freedom to a central authority, which in turn sets customs and makes laws to protect the rights of its members. Under this contract, everyone benefits. Many of these concepts are not fully grasped until well into one's twenties, and some adults never get there. We often mistakenly presume that a child has achieved the moral maturity of an adult by his teenage years. According to Michael Thompson, by eighth grade 50 percent of kids still make decisions of moral consequence based on whether they will lead to punishment.

The vast majority of teens know the difference between right and wrong. The rules they live by, however, may sometimes differ from yours. Risks are justified in the teen rulebook because that's how they learn things. In this brave new world of autonomy, teens feel a right to their own power, and they are interested in testing its limits. They may defy your rules or advice, not because they lack values and morals, but rather because they are reserving the right to sort out some things for themselves. For the time being (I know it feels like forever, but it'll last only a few years), your son's moral code is determined by the group of knuckleheads he hangs out with—not by you. A teen's morality often dictates loyalty to his peer group rather than to you or even to the society at large. At this stage he'd rather be a "good friend" than a "good boy."

Lying

Teens lie. Every one of them. Okay, that's a slight exaggeration. According to authors Bronson and Merryman, in their carefully researched book *Nurtureshock*, approximately 96 percent of teens lie. If your son is an opt-out, it's particularly unlikely he's one of the 4 percent who've never lied. Many parents have told me their child's lying bothers them. Why wouldn't it? They are honest people who want to raise ethical kids they can trust. I have met few truly dishonest people who did not know right from wrong. I can tell you with great certainty that your son is not lying because he's inherently dishonest. Nor is it a reflection of how you are parenting him.

It is obviously important to set standards for your family's ethical behavior. But you also need to understand why kids lie, so that you don't overreact. Overreacting will only make them more secretive. Lying is not just a part of growing up, but also a part of being human. Have you ever lied to anyone? I imagine that the 96 percent statistic is true for adults as well.

When your son was about two years old, he learned that he could say no, and it became his favorite word. This was his first taste of autonomy. Shortly thereafter it occurred to him that if you didn't see him break the lamp, you might not know about it. Your son lies to you as way of asserting his independence. He feels that he can handle things on his own, so the less you know the better. He also lies to stay out of trouble.

I know what you are thinking (because I think it, too): Lying only makes things worse. Not to your son, it doesn't—especially not when he gets caught with ten zeroes for homework. A seventeen-year-old patient, who was often in this position, told me: "It is the easiest thing to do at the time. I know eventually I will get caught and lectured to, but each lie I get away with postpones that lecture just a little longer." As Rosalind Wiseman, author of

Masterminds and Wingmen, points out, the personal satisfaction of being honest loses almost every time to the immediate relief a teen feels when he can avoid dealing with his parents' anger and disappointment. And kids always underestimate their chances of getting caught. Most likely, your son is going to hedge his bets and hope he gets away with it. Even if he's busted for every third offense, he is still ahead.

Keep in mind the nature of the lie: Telling you he already did his homework is very different from not telling you he dented the car. It is important to talk to your son about trust, and kids do care when they disappoint you. It may also be necessary to teach your child a lesson about owning up to and facing consequences. However, blindly trusting your son is not wise. You may think you can, but it is an illusion.

In many cases it's more important to punish your son for the offense than to worry about his efforts to cover it up. The message that lying makes things worse is often ineffective and sometimes backfires. For example, let's say he had friends over when you were out and did not tell you (why would he, since the whole point of breaking the rule is to do it behind your back?). You catch him and you ground him. However, if your policy is "your punishment will be less if you do not lie to us," you could find yourself in a bind: You come home, your son tells you he had friends over, and you say, "Thanks for being honest." Now do you ground him for only one week instead of two?

Identity Lost and Found

So much is up for grabs for the tween and teen. He doesn't know, yet, what he's really going to look like, how tall he'll grow, how athletic he'll be, not to mention what college he'll go to, what his job will be, or even his sexuality. And yet he knows that adulthood is inevitable. As your son enters puberty, he needs some way to express who he is and what he wants to become, as well as how he wants to be seen by others. He needs an identity—the thing that provides each of us with a connection to our past, gives us a sense of who we are now, and guides us to where we're going.

You know he is the same boy he has always been. You can trace aspects of his personality back to when he was a child or adolescent. But right now, he feels that he must find a whole new persona. In other words, just like his body and mind, his identity must also grow and mature. This identity needs to be robust enough to ground him in a world that has suddenly expanded. *The Wizard of Oz* had a fairy-tale ending: Dorothy promised to keep to her own backyard when searching for her heart's desire. Well, most likely, the backyard no longer satisfies a young man who aims to move beyond his parents' house, beyond even the comfortable boundaries of Samesville. In fact, as you'll discover in the next chapter, teenagers' brains are wired to seek novelty.

So teenagers experiment. As they learn new things, meet new people, and form new opinions, they try on different identities. Adolescence is one of the few times this type of experimentation is possible. The new lax bro swagger your young adolescent takes everywhere he goes is an attempt to re-create himself in an image he hopes others will buy in to. He's saying, *Let me see if this is the man I am going to become.* Ultimately he will figure out the kind of things he likes and is good at. He'll identify the people he wants to hang out with and the role he wants to play in his family and community. His answers to these questions will carry him into adulthood. A twenty-two-year-old patient of mine reflected on how this process worked for him:

"I started forming my own ideas instead of piggybacking on what everyone else thought. I remember thinking I did not like my religion. Maybe I'd go Buddhist. Then I spoke with my dad and decided to stay with Judaism. I thought about all sorts of things, from politics to teenage pregnancy. I guess I was figuring out my identity."

I remember when I was about thirteen I *had* to buy a Boone's Farm® T-shirt. (Boone's Farm is a brand of sweet alcohol produced by E. & J. Gallo® Winery.) The T-shirts were a must-have for any cool kid, although I'm not sure why. No one we knew actually drank the stuff. Boone's Farm was less a status symbol than it was a mascot. The team, in this case, was teenagers everywhere—teens who could have their own tastes and inside jokes and who could like things their parents could not understand. Part of the fun, of course, was that Boone's Farm is alcohol. Children wore shirts with animals on them, but this shirt allowed me to experiment with an adult identity.

It's important that you honor all of your son's new ventures and experiments. He needs you to see "the changed him." Support his experimentation, as long as he's being safe. Some parents draw the line at earrings; others are comfortable with tattoos. When he goes beyond your comfort level or transgresses your values, try to give him alternative ways to flex his identity muscles. Perhaps, instead of a tattoo, he can get an edgy haircut. What is important is that you do not become critical or controlling. That will only make him more committed to the thing he wants to try on, or do. Respect this process, which goes beyond how he dresses and deeper than his concern about what others think of him.

And although he would deny it, he is still watching your every move for more clues about who he is or what he will become. Being a good role model is even more critical now because, these days, your teen is observing you even more acutely than when he was younger. In just a few years' time he will have a more secure sense of himself, one that incorporates all the values you raised him with but that is also uniquely him. Don't fear—all of those values you instilled in him are still knocking around in there.

Friends

The primary way teens develop their identity is through their friends. Your son is actually much more worried about having friends and what they think than he is about his grades. This is why, as a therapist, when an opt-out also has trouble fitting in with his peers, I work on his social issues first. Since your son now looks less to you to set the bar for how he should act, feel, and think, and is not yet ready to rely on himself for this, he must turn elsewhere for validation. Here's where friends come in. Teens look to one another for clues about how to be in the world, what clothes to wear, what music to listen to, and even how to feel about school (definitely not cool). The popular kids, who have the most status, are the ones that other kids want to be liked by. I had a laugh when an eighth-grade patient described to me school gossip about who did and didn't wear Timberland® boots. Even back when I was fourteen, Timberland boots were the height of cool. That's an impressive reign. Apparently, today it's not enough to just own a pair. My patient asked if we used to scuff them, "clock" the heels, and tie them around the middle rather than all the way up.

Younger teens tend to idealize their friends the same way they did their parents. A guidance counselor I know says the favorite color of her middle school students is "beige" because everyone wants to fit in. Luckily, as teens get older, self-awareness and critical thinking help them become more discriminating.

Feelings

Adolescence is an emotional roller coaster. Teens experience feelings more intensely and deeply than both children and adults. They are uncertain about how to handle new urges and experiences, and they have powerful impulses that are sometimes beyond their control.

All the drama you are witnessing is actually a sign that your son is struggling to keep his feelings in check; the turmoil doesn't stem from his feelings—it's the way that he is managing them that is causing the turmoil. The psychological term for this is *regulation*, and it comes up a lot with the teens who opt out. Your car has a gas pedal to regulate the combustion of gasoline. A thermostat controls temperature in your house. A person's ability to regulate his feelings depends on many things and as in so many other aspects of adolescence, your son's ability to regulate his feelings grows in spurts. Here, too, he is trying to learn to manage without you. Because teens' bodies and minds are changing so dramatically, teens desperately want the world around them to be their anchor. They also often believe that the challenges and feelings they have now will last forever. That includes the good, like his elation about dating the girl his friends think is hot, and the bad, like being jettisoned from the varsity lacrosse team. We adults know the world just doesn't work like that. In fact the only thing we can count on is that nothing remains the same.

Teens need to be reminded that no one ever died from a bad feeling, and that no feeling lasts forever. Give your child some perspective the next time he is overwhelmed. Try something like: "Right now you're in the middle of a thunderstorm. Your problems may well feel all-consuming and miserable, but it never rains forever and it's not raining everywhere. At some point these clouds will pass by and you will get beyond this. Don't forget, too, that there is a reason planes fly so high: Above the clouds it's always clear. In the big picture, above the clouds, you are okay and will be okay."

Paradigm Shift

By this point, you can appreciate how profound a change it is to move from childhood to adolescence. Making this transition is difficult for everyone, as it was for even you and me. Like the proverb says: "It's difficult to decide whether growing pains are something teenagers have—or are." In order for your son to grow up, he has got to start thinking for himself, forming his own opinions, and experimenting with his own beliefs. To do all of this, he is going to need some freedom—the opportunity to wonder, muse, disagree, and get lost in thought. It's called autonomy, and the only way you can give it to him is by letting go. During adolescence, minds and bodies are not the only things that shift: Parents must also take on a new role.

Of all the changes discussed thus far, the most difficult one to bear is the shift in your own relationship with your son. He still looks up to you (though he would never admit it), but he no longer idealizes you. Each day he needs you just a little less. Michael Bradley, author of the aptly named *Yes, Your Teen Is Crazy*, put it this way: "Few of us are aware of how close we are with our children until we lose them to adolescence. We have no idea how much we have come to place our own need for nurturing and love in the hands of our kids until they shred it up and throw it in our faces." Psychologists call this process separation and individuation. I consider it more of a divestment. Your son must divest from seeing you as godlike and the sole source of his love and acceptance. Think of when Toto pulled the curtain back to reveal the Wizard of Oz. Now, I'm not suggesting that you're a fraud, but the wizard was only persuasive because the citizens of the Emerald City needed to believe in him. In order for children to grow up, they must stop believing that their parents possess magical powers and are all-powerful. Dorothy was not free to leave Oz (that is, childhood) until she saw the wizard for who he really was. As painful as this process is, and for some parents it is harder than for others, divestment is a necessary step toward self-reliance.

Parenting children of any age requires patience and restraint, but teens have the unique—and powerful—ability to suck the equilibrium out of even the most even-tempered adults. Their push for freedom is on a collision course with your need to keep them safe. Their quest for emotional distance threatens your longing to hold them close. Their assault on your personality challenges your wish to be looked up to and respected. Here are some things to keep in mind as you weather the storm of shifting roles:

DO NOT TAKE ANY OF THIS PERSONALLY. Although it may seem like it, he is not taking you for granted, rejecting you, or even hating you. He is just trying to separate. Taking things personally will lead you to feel angry, frustrated, hurt, and even guilty. It's these feelings that destroy your equilibrium, not your son.

HE IS GOING TO ACT OUT HIS AMBIVALENCE ABOUT GROWING UP MOSTLY AT HOME. That is where he will act lazy, irresponsible, and demanding. I am not telling you to just keep quiet and take it, but do not make the mistake of believing he will never grow up, or get too frustrated when none of your actions seem to help.

KNOW YOUR FEELINGS, TOLERATE THEM, BUT KEEP THEM TO YOURSELF. This is the hardest part of raising a teen. He will elicit all sorts of feelings: rage, loss, fear (and, of course, joy, pride, and amazement). Talk to your friends, your spouse, and your therapist, if need be. Don't just dump your feelings on your son.

TAKE HIM SERIOUSLY. Your son needs to know that you are hearing him. This does not mean that you have to agree with everything he says, or let him do everything he asks. But he does need you to treat him with respect, not demean his thoughts as foolish even if they are, and understand his perspective.

SET LIMITS. Your son needs as much supervision as he did a few years ago; you just need to do it in the background. He needs to know that you are around, paying attention, and ready to jump in when needed. (I will have a lot more to say about this in chapter 9.)

RESPECT HIS NEED FOR INDEPENDENCE. Taking your advice, seeking your counsel, and even going out to dinner with you threatens his autonomy. He still needs you to guide him, but not as much as when he was little. He needs to experiment and make mistakes. As long as he is safe, he will probably learn more from his bad decisions than from his good ones.

Your son's growing self-reliance is great, but there is a dark side to learning to think for yourself. Some of this darkness is easier to bear if you understand it from your son's perspective.

HE IS GOING TO THINK YOU ARE AN IDIOT. The transition from childhood to becoming an adult is a process that, during adolescence, often feels more like the swing of a pendulum than a forward progression. That sweet boy who once took your word on everything now has an overwhelming impulse to disagree with you. Mark Twain was believed to have said: "When I was a boy of fourteen, my father was so ignorant I could hardly stand to have the old man around. But when I got to be twenty-one, I was astonished at how much the old man had learned in seven years." Teens apply their new critical thinking skills to criticizing everything, including you. This is because teens, unlike children, can compare themselves with others, including their friends, teachers, and parents, and these comparisons lead them to a more realistic appraisal of themselves and others.

When your son calls your exercise routine "lame" or chastises you as being "anti-environment" because of all those plastic bags you brought home from the grocery store one time (which he did not help you unpack), take pause. Appreciate all the thinking he is doing to make sense of the world. This is a good time *not* to take things personally; he's just figuring out how to become his own person. A little self-deprecating humor will let him know you can take the poke. I once told my son that when he was little I started giving money to a charity for children whose fathers were idiots, in case he ever needed help. Look at his opinions as opportunities to get him thinking *more*, to build a stronger argument, and to get more facts.

HE'S GOING TO BE CYNICAL. Now that your son feels more comfortable challenging authority, he might also become a little skeptical or cynical. Once the ultimate authority figures, parents and teachers now appear to have flawed logic, and your son sees inconsistencies in your behavior. Whenever parents ask me how to curb their teen's cell phone addiction, I always get an uncomfortable laugh when I ask them how quickly they check their own cell phones after waking up. Kids see these things, and right now your son sees them in even greater focus. This is good; you are just modeling being human. So, with this in mind, don't be troubled by your son's cynicism.

HE'S GOING TO CHALLENGE AUTHORITY. Tyler, a high school junior, was recently assigned *The Tao of Pooh*, Benjamin Hoff's whimsical introduction to Eastern philosophy. Tyler's takeaway was: "I think my school follows Confucianism, but I wish they were more into Tao." What he meant was that his school expects students to obediently subscribe to and follow the wisdom of their teachers, rather than encouraging independent thought. In order to reach this conclusion, Tyler had to understand the basic (abstract) principles of each belief system, and then compare and contrast these principles. I didn't point out that the joke was on him: It was his school's wonderful curriculum and teaching that taught him to be a critical thinker in the first place.

HE'S GOING TO BE OPINIONATED. There is nothing more passionate than a teenager expressing a new belief or viewpoint. However, teens are also relentless. Living with a zealot is never easy. Teens can overdo it because they need to separate and are insecure about their opinions and conclusions. Shakespeare could have had a defensive teenager in mind when he wrote Hamlet's famous line "Methinks she does protest too much." Teens are fighting the urge to still rely upon you to tell them how to think. For a time, they need to build up their own perspectives by knocking everyone else's down (at least everyone who is over the age of seventeen). So forgive your son if he is a little too brash or strident. (Anyway, if they are going to fix all of our mistakes, young people need to be a little idealistic.)

HE'S GOING TO BE SELFISH. Teens are self-centered, and parents and siblings often feel left in the dust. Perhaps you are thinking this contradicts the earlier notion of developing empathy in adolescence. Remember, his mind is not changing all at once. Empathy takes times to develop, and some people are better at it than others. For now, your son's newfound ability to imagine himself from the perspective of others is most often used in the service of figuring out who he is.

Focus on the opt-out

The opt-out is like any other teen, only more so. He seems behind schedule—the developmental time line that culminates in college and independence that every parent keeps in their head. However, *behind* is really a misnomer. There are some areas where he is ahead, and others where he is right on target. Unfortunately, the problem comes from his and your emotional reactions to this unevenness.

All teens harbor secret and serious doubts about making it in the real world. Remember, beneath a facade of fearlessness and risk taking is often a kid who feels vulnerable and afraid. However, the challenges of adolescence are more confusing for the opt-out, who is generally insecure and anxious and does not yet have the confidence that he'll be able to grow up. The transition from dependence to independence is simply too complicated for him and, as a result, for you. He is immobilized—stuck in the middle of a bridge or stranded like debris in a whirlpool. Your son may never show those feelings to anyone because that would expose the dependency he is desperately trying to shed. So he adopts an I-don't-care attitude about school and withdraws. He will insist on independence, and want the rewards of adulthood, but stubbornly refuse to take responsibility for the things that will actually help him progress, like decent grades. He will also fight your every attempt to nudge him forward.

The opt-out's problems intertwine with normal teenage development (a problem in its own right) to make one big knot. We are untangling it a thread at a time. Your son may have a heavier dose of ambivalence than the average teen, but his struggle toward self-reliance is not unique. All adolescent boys rely on avoidance to manage their anxiety, but the opt-out carries it too far. Let's shine a spotlight on two other aspects of development, to learn how they impact your son.

THE UNEVEN PATH OF DEVELOPMENT

Development's path is never straight. There are false starts and logjams, smooth roads that lead to hairpin curves, and potholes everywhere. Everyone gets through adolescence, but no one goes through it exactly the same way.

This is especially true for the opt-out. While every boy develops according to his own unique timetable, the opt-out trails behind in one or more areas. These areas, which I'll discuss in detail, include maturity, thinking, executive skills, and self-regulation. Simply put, he is not ready to grow up. Rest assured, however, that your opt-out will get there. He'll blossom, he'll grow, his mind will expand, and his judgment will improve. It might take some time—maybe more than you think he can afford—but his pace is out of your control. You cannot speed up development, and no amount of coaching, tutoring, or therapy will overpower his DNA. Not only do many opt-outs develop more slowly than their peers (and I am speaking less about physical than cognitive and emotional development), their growth is also uneven. Accepting this will change how you view your opt-out. When you consider his lack of engagement as less a matter of will and more an effect of brain development, you'll be better equipped to make the paradigm shift discussed in chapter 1 (see page 36) and, in turn, become a more effective parent. You cannot hasten your son's development.

Here are some examples of a teen's uneven cognitive development:

- He may be able to understand concepts better than he can articulate them.
- He may be able to remember facts or names better than numbers.
- He may be a slow reader, even though his comprehension skills are excellent.
- He may be a whiz when it comes to history but unable to read between the lines of a novel or poem.
- He may have a keen intellect but produce work very slowly

because it takes longer for information to transfer from one part of his brain to another.

- He may understand the difference between a novel's theme and plot, but not between mass and volume.

Most likely the unevenness that has the biggest impact on your son's learning is in the area of executive functioning. (See chapter 4, which focuses exclusively on this issue.)

WHEN OPTING OUT BECOMES YOUR TEEN'S IDENTITY

For many of the opt-outs I have met, *being a school avoider becomes one of the identities they try on.* This identity is not, however, about projecting a fantasy of their future self; it's about self-protection. Children will protect their self-esteem at all costs. While some kids respond to the pressures of school by working harder, your son is too afraid he will fail, which would be too big a blow to his self-worth.

He might have struggled one way or another in school since he was young. Maybe he has ADHD (attention deficit hyperactivity disorder), which has affected his ability to work consistently. Maybe he is uneven in all of the ways we've discussed thus far—his road is still a little bumpy and he hasn't yet figured out how to chart a smoother, more effective course. So he develops an identity that is not so much about trying new things as it is about preserving his self-worth. This is the identity of the opt-out. He is "too cool for school."

While this identity may protect him from trying and failing, ultimately it keeps him from doing all of the experimenting and risk taking that is so critical for a teen's development. Perhaps he is one of those opt-outs like Mr. Popular (see page 11) who can put himself out there in other ways, be it socially, athletically, or in another extracurricular pursuit. This type of opt-out usually finds his way. However, many of the boys I have worked with are as shut down outside of school as they are in the classroom. There is hope for these boys, but their problems are going to take a bit longer to solve.

Ultimately your son is going to have to take responsibility for himself, so let's help him figure out how to get unstuck, stop fighting with you so much, and find his own competence so that he will have the confidence to one day make it on his own.

3

If I Only Had a Brain

I wish I'd had a time machine so that at twenty I could have gone back to my sixteen-year-old self and told him what an idiot he was being.

—JONAH PRICE, AGE TWENTY-THREE

George's arrest was merely at the crest of a wave of bad decisions he had recently made. On the fateful day that he was taken into police custody, this otherwise smart and likable seventeen-year-old took care to park his parents' minivan at the far end of the hockey rink's parking lot. He knew how rowdy the crowd would be after the big game between his high school and a local rival, and he didn't want to risk being sideswiped. George made sure all the windows were rolled up and that the car was locked. However, the open bottle of vodka he'd left on the front seat was in clear view of an officer, and George was arrested as soon as he and his friends returned to the car.

Later, George told me he could not believe his stupidity. "Everyone," he said, "knows that police presence is strong during high school hockey games." I explained to George something that scientists have known for some time: The teenage brain is uniquely geared to experience pleasure and seek novelty. Unfortunately for George, during adolescence this part of the brain is not yet wired into the control center, the section that thinks ahead, makes plans, and generally slows things down. George's reaction to this news? "I cannot wait for *that* to happen."

The last chapter focused on the upheaval created by the dramatic changes happening to the body, mind, and emotions of your teenager. Now we'll take a look under the hood at the engine that is powering all of these changes. This neuroscientific tour will illuminate the fact that teenagers are, more than we ever realized, works in progress. A teenager's brain, as Dr. Abigail Baird noted, is as gawky as his body. New research has dismantled many myths about adolescent development, the greatest one being that teens are just small adults. The recognition that your son's brain is substantially different from yours will help you to understand his erratic behavior and, more important, manage your expectations. This, in turn, will generate patience, a much-needed commodity for the parents of opt-outs, yet one that is often found in woefully short supply.

A revolution in adolescent brain research has also shattered the myth that sex hormones are the cause of all teenage turmoil. While testosterone and estrogen definitely play a leading role, they also trigger a major phase of brain development. Previously it was believed that there was only one such major stage—from birth to age three, after which changes in the brain were thought to happen incrementally. Now we know that, starting with puberty, a second major reorganization occurs, and this one lasts well into young adulthood. According to the eminent psychologist Laurence Steinberg, and other investigators of adolescent development, puberty now starts as early as age ten, and it's not officially finished until age twenty-six!

The Changing Brain

One of the most amazing things about the human brain is that it is never quiet. I'm not talking about the seemingly endless parade of thoughts we all have. Rather, I'm referring to changes the brain experiences on a molecular level that occur throughout our lifetimes, even when we're sleeping. The simple word for this is *learning*. However, neuroscientists have another name for it— *plasticity*. Probably for reasons related to our survival, the brain is programmed to go through critical periods where these changes are more profound.

We have always known that teens are particularly impressionable, and now we know why: Their brains are uniquely malleable, which helps them to answer questions such as "Who am I?" and "Who will I become?" It also eventually allows them to become more mature, logical, and thoughtful. For this reason, adolescence has been termed the Age of Opportunity and Golden Age of Innovation. In the words of Frances Jensen, author of *The Teenage Brain*, teens have "a short window to experience the world and figure out what will make them happier, healthier, and, one can only hope, wiser." Of course, the downside to all of this openness is that teens are keenly vulnerable to risks such as addiction, stress, and perhaps even opting out.

A NEW FRONTIER

Until recently, the brain was not an easy thing to study. Neuroscience relied mainly on animal experiments and single case studies of people who were either dead or victims of disease or trauma. The most famous of these dates back to a tragic accident in 1848 involving Phineas Gage, a twenty-five-year-old railroad-crew foreman. While Gage was using a thirteen-and-a-half-pound tamping iron to pack explosive powder into a hole, the powder ignited somehow and launched the iron rod into his left cheek, through his brain, and out of his skull, landing onto the ground a few feet away! Gage not only survived but, later that day, uttered a statement to his doctor that is now well known to anyone who has studied neuropsychology: "Here is business enough for you." The observations of the town doctor who saved Gage's life allowed brain scientists to draw the first connection between brain injury and personality. In this case, the rod took with it a good chunk of Gage's prefrontal cortex, leaving him unable to plan ahead or control his impulses. In other words, Phineas Gage gave us the first clue about executive functions.

Although studies like this one (admittedly, most are less dramatic) taught us much about the brain, there was no way to conduct a controlled study with healthy people or learn how the brain changes over time. However, in the past fifteen years nothing short of a revolution has taken place, thanks to new technology and the work of pioneering researchers such as Dr. Jay Giedd, Dr. B. J. Casey, and Dr. Abigail Baird. With the advent of magnetic resonance imaging (MRI), brain activity can be measured in healthy, normal teens who do nothing more than lie still. While an MRI can take a detailed picture of what is going on, functional magnetic resonance imaging (fMRI) acts more like a movie camera that captures which parts of the brain "switch on" during an activity. It does so by measuring the oxygen level in blood that the brain absorbs when in action. For example, we can tell how a teen's brain reacts when he looks at a picture of someone crying versus an image of someone eating an ice cream cone.

Dr. Giedd and his colleagues at the National Institute of Mental Health (NIMH) were the first to conduct a longitudinal study of children and adults using this scanning technology. In 1999, when they first reported their result, the playing field was small—only about four hundred papers were published that year on neuroimaging with children. By 2010, however, the number grew to fourteen hundred journal articles! We now know that the brain develops over many decades, and we also have a much better understanding of how its different regions are connected. To understand these findings, a crash course in brain anatomy is required.

Brain Development 101

There is nothing black and white about how the brain develops—it's actually gray and white. The gray matter of the brain is made up of a hundred billion nerve cells called neurons. In order for the brain and nervous system to work, these cells have to be able to send and receive signals, much like a phone system (the one attached to your wall, not the one in your pocket). At the neurons' center is the cell body, which contains the nucleus. This is the command center of the cell or, using the previous metaphor, the phone itself. Short branches called dendrites grow out of the cell body, and these dendrites receive signals from other cells. Each neuron has up to a hundred thousand dendrites, which produce even smaller twigs.

White matter is made up of axons: long nerve fibers that send signals from one brain cell to another. There is only one axon per neuron, but each axon has its own branches. Going back to the phone system comparison, axons and dendrites are the wires that make the connections between individual phones.

Here is where it gets interesting: The brain is flexible because axons and dendrites do not physically attach to each other. Rather, when a connection is needed to relay specific information, a gap, known as a synapse, is formed between these two junctions. This gap is then traversed by a neurotransmitter, which is an electrically charged chemical. So it's not a metaphor to say that the brain is "wired"—it's a literal statement. There are upward of a hundred different types of these chemicals; no one knows the exact number. And many of these neurotransmitters are specialized to accept signals from a specific neurotransmitter. Each neurotransmitter may have different receptor cells based upon the job it is doing.

Adenosine is one such neurotransmitter. It's probably your son's second favorite. (His first is dopamine—more on that soon.) Adenosine is part of the brain's sleep mechanism. When the brain produces this neurotransmitter, it binds to its receptors to slow down cell activity and make us sleepy. However, nature has produced something that is adenosine's chemical twin—caffeine. Caffeine, in essence, tricks the adenosine receptors to bind with it, thus blocking the real thing from lulling us into dreamland. Most psychiatric medications work on the same principle. The selective serotonin reuptake inhibitors (SSRIs), which you might know as Prozac®, Zoloft®, or Lexapro®, alleviate anxiety and depression by acting like a dam. They bind with the receptor cells that absorb serotonin and, in turn, allow that serotonin the brain has already produced to stay active for a longer period of time.

The network—cell body → dendrite → synapse → neurotransmitter → axon → cell body—is called a neural pathway. Every thought you have, feeling you experience, or action you initiate can be understood as a series of neurons that communicate with one another through the language of electrical messaging. Practice throwing a baseball, playing the violin, or memorizing the periodic table and you are activating thousands of specific neural pathways. The more you do these things, the more the connections are strengthened. This puts that old adage "Practice makes perfect" in a whole new light. Furthermore, every time you learn something, the brain creates more synapses and receptors. The number of possible brain pathways is . . . well, I'll let you do the math: one hundred billion neurons times up to ten thousand possible connections. In fact, if every neuron in the brain of a human at birth were connected with every other neuron, a typical newborn's brain would have to be as large as Manhattan. Fortunately, nature has solved this problem by ensuring that we will never need that much wiring.

AN EVOLUTIONARY PATH

The brain is uniquely designed to adapt to its environment. While human development follows a pre-programmed genetic path, there is lots of room for customization. This allows us to develop the skills and abilities we need to survive, both as individuals and, more important, as a species. So instead of coming "fully loaded," an infant is born with some essential features, as well as the potential to develop the optimal skills for its environment. This is why babies are born with many more neurons than they need, but with very little wiring.

Many brain scientists believe that brain development follows an evolutionary path, from the most primitive to the most complex, or literally from the bottom up. The bottom regions of the brain are the quickest to develop since they control life's most basic functions: breathing, sleeping, heart rate, temperature, balance, and alerting caregivers to hunger, thirst, or discomfort. Now get ready for a little science fiction: These brain structures (the brain stem and cerebellum) have been called "the reptilian brain," because they resemble the entirety of your pet turtle or chameleon's brain. Connections from the sensory and motor areas in a newborn's brain are quickly formed with other regions. A child's brain is groomed to walk, talk, and then develop fine motor skills (grasping, holding, et cetera), all within the first critical period of life. While your son was peacefully asleep in his crib, his brain was forming two million synapses every second!

Once these skills are acquired, the brain "seals" them in by losing its plasticity in the related regions. This "hardening" ensures that these functions will remain stable throughout a lifetime; we do not need to become better at breathing or seeing, we just need to be able to do it. However, more complex brain functions like judgment and planning take much longer to develop.

To understand how this amazing process happens, let's switch to the metaphor of a computer. The brain has almost all of the hardware (gray matter) it needs by age six. By then, the brain has reached 90 percent of its adult size. It's the skull that keeps growing. After that, brain development is all about reorganization. Think of this reorganization as a series of software upgrades that are necessary to get the most of out of the complex hardware, which, by the way, also includes our nervous system and body. These upgrades happen gradually throughout childhood. Then puberty ushers in the metaphorical installation of a new operating system—one that allows for a leaner and meaner brain.

LEANER

During childhood the brain produces more synapses and neural connections than it really needs. Throughout life the brain pares down the unnecessary connections, much the way a gardener prunes a bush, cutting back dispensable leaves and branches so that the essential ones can thrive.

Recent brain research revealed that pruning peaks during adolescence. This is major. Although new and very significant connections continue to be made, the teenage brain is kept extremely busy discarding unneeded baggage before it makes the big transition to adulthood. Giedd discovered that, particularly in the frontal lobe (more on that brain region in chapter 4), the volume of gray matter increases during childhood and early adolescence, tops out at age twelve, and then begins to decline. During adolescence, the brain loses 7 to 10 percent of its gray area and in some spots up to 50 percent. Don't panic; your son is not losing any brainpower. His brain is becoming streamlined.

MEANER

The brain becomes much more efficient through a process called myelination. Myelin is a white fatty substance that has been likened to insulation. It coats axons, making the transmission of information as much as one hundred times faster. At birth, only a baby's brain stem (the place where automatic functions like breathing occur) is fully myelinated. This lack of myelination accounts for a baby's slow reaction times. As more and more regions of the brain become connected, myelin plays as central role in quickly getting information where it needs to go. Myelin is critical to a brain that can respond and react to potential threats, as well as solve complex problems.

We now know that myelination plays a significant role in brain development. In essence, as the gray in a child's brain becomes whiter and whiter, the brain's connections become stronger and better insulated. The massive reorganization of the adolescent brain consists primarily of pruning and myelination. However, as Steinberg points out, the real significance "is not the fact that remodeling is taking place, but where it is happening."

Emotion Over Mind

Development during the first period of life follows a fairly consistent path: Most babies develop in the same way, according to the same timetable. It really doesn't make any difference if your child was the first of his peers to be toilet-trained or the last to walk. And barring some significant problem, everyone eventually learns to talk. Adolescent brain development, in comparison, is not nearly as predictable or consistent. There is greater variation in the skills and abilities that emerge during the teen years, including language facility, logical reasoning, planning, and self-control.

All of those *charming* characteristics we associate with adolescence—impulsiveness, moodiness, unpredictability, and so on—are really just the result of asymmetrical development. Your son is not just an adult with less experience and poor decision-making skills. He has a very different brain than you have, one that is primed for novelty, craves excitement, and lures him out of the secure nest you've built for him. The part of his brain that provides a "second sober thought" lags far behind.

The difference between an adolescent brain and an adult one is found in the limbic system, the part of the brain that controls feelings and reactions. By adolescence the limbic system, programmed to explode at puberty, is not yet well connected to the prefrontal cortex, the part of the brain that plans, controls impulses, and curbs antisocial behavior. Not only does the brain develop from the bottom up, but the processes of myelination and pruning start at the back of the brain and make their way forward; so the prefrontal cortex, located way up front in the brain above the eyebrows, must wait. All that complexity takes time to develop— approximately twenty-five years! Hence adolescence.

Now pause for a moment to think about your son. Recall some of the antics he and his friends have pulled. Reflect on how out of proportion his emotional reactions seem sometimes and on how sensitive he can be. Given all the aforementioned facts about brain development, not to mention that the settle-down-and-get-to-work part of his brain isn't yet up and running, you can understand why so many experts on adolescents have described them as sports cars without brakes.

The Feeling and Reacting Brain

Fortunately, only a small portion of our brains is lizard-like. The next stage in the human brain's evolution is called paleomammalian. This stage, which elevates us (metaphorically) from reptiles to mammals, marks the development of the limbic system. What is so fascinating is that our system of emotions originates in memory. Our long-term memories are stored in a sea-horse-shaped structure called the hippocampus (which is Latin for "sea horse"). Right next to the hippocampus is a structure that draws its name from the Latin word for "almond"—the amygdala. Don't be fooled by its size. This very small "nut" packs a wallop. The amygdala's main job is to be the brain's gatekeeper. It's where our "gut" feelings come from. The amygdala assesses new situations for danger and, if necessary, gives the order to fight or flee. So the hippocampus stores information about what experiences are agreeable or disagreeable, and then it helps the amygdala sort out what to do. This type of emotional learning, another example of the brain's plasticity, is central to our self-preservation. Our brains store experiences and use them to avoid potential threats, such as lions, tigers, and bears; the gathered information also helps to inform the brain about potentially rewarding situations—like, for your son, the "hottie" he hopes to ask to prom. A precise (and perhaps uncomfortable for you) word for this is *arousal*, which brings us back to your teenager. Dr. Frances Jensen, author of *The Teenage Brain*, puts it this way: "A slightly unbridled and over-exuberant immature amygdala is thought to contribute to adolescent explosiveness."

Hormones

After all this talk about wiring and insulation, we can discuss something a little more familiar—hormones. Unlike neurotransmitters, which are produced by neurons and unique to the brain, hormones are produced by the endocrine system (think glands) and travel through the entire body. During puberty, the pituitary gland—kind of like the brain's pharmacy—releases hormones that significantly impact the limbic system. These hormones—particularly adrenaline, which is linked to the fight-or-flight syndrome, and the "sex" hormones testosterone and estrogen—cause an emotional intensity that is uniquely adolescent.

Teens process emotions differently than do adults, and testosterone is partly to blame. Puberty raises a boy's testosterone levels by up to 30 percent, and during adolescence the amygdala cannot seem to get enough of this stuff, as it becomes awash with receptors for the hormone. This is why teen boys are so prone to aggressive outbursts . . . and like to fight. An amped-up amygdala means that teens are more likely to misinterpret a sideways glance or overreact when their girlfriend talks to another boy. Add a little alcohol to the mix and the results can be disastrous.

However, there is an even more significant difference between how teens and adults interpret potentially dangerous situations. There are two different routes information can travel to get to the amygdala, one scenic and the other direct. The scenic route winds through the frontal cortex. There are metaphorical curves in the road—like reason, reflection, and impulse control—that serve as filters and slow things down. The teenage need for speed (perception → emotion → reaction, wham, bam, pow) is explained by the fact that the neural pathways between an adolescent's limbic system and prefrontal cortex are immature. Put another way, the scenic route is under construction.

This prefrontal cortex bypass was one of the first findings to emerge from fMRI studies of the teenage brain. Abigail Baird, who coined the term *neural gawkiness*, and her colleagues at McLeans Hospital found that when adults were hooked up to an fMR and shown pictures of men looking fearful, their frontal cortexes lit up. Not so for adolescents, whose amygdalas rocked the scanner when shown the same picture. Why, you may wonder, did that particular image evoke such different results? A fearful expression represents a threat even more than an angry one, and the brain must quickly decide if the threat is real or perceived.

This is why there are two routes from the limbic system to the prefrontal cortex. Something as scary as a lion chasing you will trigger the direct route. However, under more ambiguous circumstances, the brain needs a screening process before engaging in a fight or running away. This research suggests that teens don't screen as well as adults do. Even more frightening is the finding that younger teens actually misperceive emotions and, for example, label fear as anger. The conclusion? A teen's bad judgment might really be about how he processes emotions. That and dopamine.

Dopamine

Among neurotransmitters, dopamine has a celebrity status because it's all about sex, drugs, and rock 'n' roll. One of its many jobs in the brain is to motivate us to seek out pleasurable experiences. Alcohol and drugs such as cocaine and heroin mimic dopamine (kind of like caffeine and adenosine), which is one of the reasons they make people feel good—and why they can be addictive. So do sex and that piece of chocolate cake you've been resisting all day. That piece of cake serves as a cue—it triggers activity in the neural pathways that rely on dopamine, and once those pathways are activated they want to keep on firing. Dopamine is all about desire and delight.

Although society has a few things to say about it, in terms of reproduction, once a human being achieves sexual maturity and is fertile, it is all-systems-go. This may have something to do with why during puberty there is an increase in the number of dopamine receptors in a small structure within the limbic system called the nucleus accumbens. Referring to the effect of dopamine on the teenage brain, Barbara Strauch, who wrote one of the first books on the new frontier of adolescent brain research, says, "Teenagers may be walloped with an outsized, almost psychedelic view of the world around them—reds are redder; blues are bluer. Their world may be more aglow, more exuberant . . . Dopamine may be painting walls of the mind bright purple, turning up the inner radio and goading 'Go grab it, Do something! Jump.'"

To meet the demands of all these dopamine receptors crying out "Feed me, feed me," teens are almost involuntarily drawn to stimulation. Nothing gives them more of a rush than taking a risk. Thankfully, risks are not all bad. In fact, it's a combination of greater brain plasticity and a heightened sensitivity to dopamine that makes adolescence the Age of Opportunity. Adolescents are primed to learn new things quickly and explore the world. Of course, there are some risks you hope your son takes on, like trying out for the debate or soccer team, and others you want him to steer clear of.

Laurence Steinberg has studied teens and risk. His extensive research found that, surprisingly, teens are no worse than adults in evaluating the risk in a given situation. It isn't necessarily poor judgment that leads them to trouble. Rather, teenagers use a different scale to measure risk and reward: one in which the reward side is unfairly weighted by all of those dopamine receptors. Dr. Steinberg explains, "Compared to children and adults, adolescents are more likely to approach situations in which they think a reward may be likely, but they are less likely to avoid situations in which they think they may have something to lose." This bias is something that parents and teachers should keep in mind: It's easier to change an adolescent's behavior by motivating him with the prospect of a reward than by threatening him with a potential punishment.

Paradigm Shift

This is more than a paradigm shift—it's a major sea change. When your son was three and needed to take a nap, you did not call him lazy. You knew he was still growing, and napping was just a part of development. Well, things are no different now that he is a teenager (including the nap), but since he looks and sounds like an adult, you think he should act like one. However, his brain is structurally different from yours (or those of his younger brothers and sisters). To throw you even more off the track, he actually seems to get it— sometimes he remembers to flush the toilet or asks if you've had a hard day. But don't be fooled: Development occurs in fits and starts. Chances are you were much more immature at his age than you remember—especially if you are a dad. I know I was.

I have shared with you some of the most important context that explains why your teenage son can be so sensitive, dramatic, or imprudent. I've discussed the roles that both the limbic system and emotion play in the motivation for self-preservation. This is very different, however, from the motivation to excel in school. The excitement and novelty your son craves does not come in the form of doing his biology lab or history paper. If anything, the role the limbic system plays in your son's opting out is to lure him away from his studies, not toward them. In order to be productive, make better choices, and harness all of that emotional energy, your son needs a voice of reason and calm—the voice of his prefrontal context. Unfortunately teens tend to leap before they look.

4

Leap Before You Look

Each year the Darwin Awards are bestowed upon people who tragically, but comically, leaped before they looked. The awards, named for the granddaddy of natural selection, purport to "improve the human genome by honoring those who accidentally removed themselves from it." A recent winner tried to rob a gun store, at gunpoint. Somehow he failed to register the police car parked outside and the security guard stationed at the door. He was also undeterred by customers milling about, many of whom were packing heat. When this Darwin recipient randomly fired his pistol . . . well, let's just say it was the last shot he took. Then there is the man who tied a copper wire to his kite's string so it would fly higher. The experience became truly electrifying when the kite got tangled in a power line. I came across a worthy candidate for the award on a trip to Yellowstone National Park with my family. Directly below a sign reading KEEP A SAFE DISTANCE FROM THE BISON, the man leaned in close to one of the beautiful, but very dangerous, beasts for a selfie.

Each of these hapless guys clearly had a goal in mind, and all neglected to think through the course of his actions. They lacked common sense *and* judgment. When psychologists talk about a voice of reason, they are referring to a collective set of brain processes called the executive functions, located right behind your eyebrows, in the brain's prefrontal cortex. This area is commonly referred to as the frontal lobes. While we know *where* they are, defining *what* they are is not so easy. At a national conference I recently attended, even the world's experts couldn't agree on a definition. Part of the problem is that the brain functions neuropsychologists actually measure—*initiate, sustain, shift*, and *inhibit*—seem a far cry from the uniquely human capacities they afford us, like *judgment* and *impulse control*. With executive functions, the whole equals far more than the sum of its parts.

Things get more complicated when you realize that by trying to make the concept more accessible, educators and psychologist have oversimplified what executive functions mean and how they work. There is some value in translating *initiate, shift, sustain*, and *inhibit* into familiar abilities such as planning, organization, and study skills; the danger here, however, is that if you apply watered-down definitions to your son's situation, you run the risk of oversimplifying his problems and, in turn, reaching for ineffective solutions. So before I take you on a tour of the prefrontal cortex and suggest some remedies that might actually work, it's time for another paradigm shift. To get it started, let's break down a few more myths.

Myth Busters

MYTH 1: EXECUTIVE FUNCTIONS ARE SKILLS THAT CAN BE TAUGHT

Executive functioning coaches now abound and, while many are helpful, their utility often ends when they leave your son's side because many of the "skills" these coaches strive to boost are automatic brain functions over which he has no control. In addition, a teenager's prefrontal cortex is still developing. As you'll recall from chapter 3, this is the last region of the brain to be pruned, myelinated, and fully connected to the rest of the brain. In other words, the brain's software cannot be upgraded until its hardware is in place.

What's more, adolescents are often not mature enough to take responsibility for applying skills they have learned to every day life.

MYTH 2: YOUR OPT-OUT NEEDS TO BE MORE ORGANIZED

Well, he probably does, but this is not the root of his problem. Parents and teachers believe that if kids were more efficient they could handle everything thrown at them. A teen is not a mini executive, and you were probably not as organized as you think you were when you were your son's age. Reducing the problem to a neat backpack or carefully updated assignment book, for instance, is another oversimplification.

MYTH 3: IF YOUR SON ONLY TRIED HARDER, HE WOULD SOLVE THIS PROBLEM

There is a difference between *can't* and *won't*, and it's crucial for you to accept that there's a lot more *can't* than *won't* going on. Part of the *can't* stems from a lack of confidence (see chapter 12), but a good chunk of it comes from an undeveloped or weak prefrontal cortex.

You Don't Know What You've Got Till It's Gone

Perhaps the easiest way to understand how executive functions work is to observe when they don't. Imagine yourself in a large grocery store. You haven't made a list and cannot remember what's lacking in your refrigerator and pantry. You also can't think ahead to what you want to make for dinner and thus can't buy the necessary ingredients. So you wander aimlessly through the aisles as the cart fills with whatever catches your fancy: cookies, a new brand of potato chips, canned soup. And then you come to the dairy section and remember you are out of milk! As one patient said, "I can't go grocery shopping unless I'm hungry."

Opt-outs are often challenged by weak or underdeveloped executive functions. Take a look at this list of problems to see if any apply to your son. Keep in mind that while a diagnosis of attention deficit hyperactive disorder is often accompanied by executive function deficits, these deficits alone do not justify the diagnosis:

- Has difficulty staying focused, especially when an assignment or job is boring or challenging.
- Does not do today what he can put off until tomorrow.
- Needs a kick in the pants to get started on something that seems boring or difficult.
- Has no time sense, underestimates how long things will take, and is often late.
- Has a poor sense of priorities.
- Finds transitions from one activity to another to be stressful.
- Hesitates or outright refuses to stop doing something he likes (like playing a video game).
- Forgets to take out the trash, turn in his homework, or pick his brother up from school.
- Loses things frequently.
- Has a messy backpack, desk, and locker.
- Work is often rushed, careless, and sloppy.
- Can only think of one way to solve a problem—even if it's the wrong way.
- Does not complete tasks or long-term assignments.
- Some days he is on fire, others he seems stalled.

- Sweats the small stuff: gets easily frustrated or overwhelmed.
- Is impatient.
- Lacks self-awareness and can be clueless about other people's feelings.
- Does not plan ahead or anticipate possible problems.
- Is unmotivated (especially with regard to things he does not want to do, like homework).

The Thinking Brain

Two million years of evolution have increased the mass of the human brain threefold. But our brains didn't just get bigger— they got better. The frontal lobes, which are the seat of reason, were the last to develop. While it is tempting to call this region the most important part of the brain, keep in mind that a quarterback needs a whole team to win a football game. It might be fair, though, to say that "the thinking brain" is what makes us human. A little comparative anatomy lends support to this statement. The frontal lobes, considered collectively, are the largest single structure, accounting for 40 percent of the human brain. As much as my family loves our dog Lilah, her prefrontal cortex comes in at only 7 percent! I am sorry for you cat lovers, but as a species, they trail behind dogs in the arena of frontal lobes (3.5 percent). As far as the rest of the animal kingdom goes, a chimp's prefrontal cortex runs a distant second to ours at 17 percent. It is actually the prefrontal cortex that coordinates the efforts of all other brain activity, all hundred million of those neurons. For this reason, the prefrontal cortex has often been likened to the conductor of a symphony. Dr. Thomas Brown, one of the leading experts on attention deficit hyperactive disorder, uses the analogy clearly:

Imagine a symphony orchestra in which each musician can play his or her instrument very well. If there is no conductor to activate and organize the orchestra so that all are playing their respective parts of the same score, and all are on the same beat; if there is not someone to signal the introduction of woodwinds or to control the fading of the stings; if the efforts of the individual musicians are not integrated and regulated by a competent conductor, the orchestra will not practice good music.

Achieving Goals

Like the many musicians in a professional orchestra, the executive functions are so well integrated with one another (and the rest of the brain) that we think of them as having a unitary purpose. This purpose is self-regulation, which is critical to the success of the individual and the species. Self-regulation allows each of us to direct our behavior toward the accomplishment of a short-term goal, be it baking a cake, writing an English paper, or preparing a legal argument. It also affords us the necessary self-control to make choices that serve our long-term best interests. The prefrontal cortex allows us to form goals and objectives, and then to devise and implement a plan to meet them. In other words, it enables us to:

- Summon relevant experiences and knowledge from memory.
- Simulate "if-then" scenarios in our minds to assess any risks and work out any kinks.
- Stay focused.
- Implement a plan in a tenable order.

- Pay attention to the current, changing landscape in case we have to alter the course of action.
- Postpone any intense emotional reactions or impulses until a goal is met.
- Evaluate the outcome.

The Executive Functions

As we now take a closer look at the executive functions, keep in mind that while each executive function operates independently, there is a lot of overlap among the functions themselves, as well as the capacities they support.

WORKING MEMORY plays a role in almost everything we do. The name, however, is misleading. It is not a form of memory—rather it's a holding cell that keeps track of the information we need in order to complete a task. In its simplest form, this includes things like remembering the fourth item on a grocery list while deciding what brand of toilet paper to buy. Working memory's importance in learning can't be understated. For your son to take notes in class, one part of his brain must keep listening while another part (working memory) remembers what his teacher said just long enough to write it down. Understanding what you read requires using working memory to keep track of facts, people, or characters introduced early on, but not mentioned again until later.

Working memory's job is not only to hold information, but also to find it. This is why it is so crucial to problem solving and critical thinking—it helps us to summon vital knowledge and previous experiences that are relevant to a task at hand. That Darwin Award–winning kite flier might still be alive today if he recalled his fourth-grade lesson on electricity. Working memory is where the "if-then" scenarios are simulated, and it's where the brain keeps a running list of the order in which things are done.

RESPONSE CONTROL. Going with your first impulse is not always the best idea. It's much better to go through life with a drop-down menu that lists possible responses to any given situation. Having this kind of choice requires time to think, something that can only happen when a person inhibits his first impulse. In fact, psychologists measure response control by testing people's ability to inhibit an automatic response: looking at a list of color names that are printed in different-colored inks ("red" is printed in blue ink, for example) and naming the ink color rather than reading the word.

Response control plays a central role in the ability to pay attention and focus. People who are easily distracted can't stop themselves from responding to many of the things that go on around them. Response control also plays a key role in judgment—it gives us time to think through our actions. Civilizations have been built on an exponential number of pauses that allowed the opportunity to think things through or change direction. On the other hand, a lack of response control has caused unfathomable tragedies throughout history.

EMOTIONAL CONTROL is not about what we feel, but rather about how we react to what we feel. It permits us to experience emotions without becoming overwhelmed or carried away by them. As discussed in chapter 3, either information can travel directly to the amygdala, where the brain's instant fight-or-flight response is centered, or it can take a detour through the executive system. This detour provides the opportunity to slow down and think of the best possible reaction: *Do I really want to leap? Better take a look first.* A toddler who throws himself on the ground and starts screaming is unable to regulate his anger and frustration, largely due to the immaturity of his frontal lobes.

The emotions that are typically the most difficult to manage include anger, frustration, disappointment, sensitivity to criticism, and desire. These feelings can quickly become all-consuming and, for those who have trouble regulating their emotions, these feelings are particularly difficult to put in perspective.

STARTING, STOPPING, AND SHIFTING. For most people, starting something they don't really want to do is a challenge—for the opt-out it's all but impossible. Effective task initiation involves emotional control, as well as time management and self-monitoring. And often, starting something you don't want to do means stopping something you are enjoying. In today's digital world the distractions are endless. Kids with ADHD tend to "hyperfocus" on things they enjoy; they become completely absorbed in something and tune out everything else. Pulling such a boy away from his favorite video game may require the same kind of epic battle he is currently waging on the screen.

Shifting, which refers to the transition between stopping and starting, allows us the flexibility to change an approach to problem solving when the one being used isn't working—say, if you have ever stripped the threads on a bolt because it was too tight, but you kept on turning it. It also enables us to revise our initial assumptions and alter course, if necessitated by a change in circumstances.

Shifting is a major component of "thinking out of the box" because it allows us to look at problems from a different perspective. Middle school and young high school students love to play a riddle game, which encourages them to challenge their basic assumptions about "the facts." The next time you are stuck in traffic, give this conundrum to your kids, which they can solve by asking you yes-or-no questions: "A man running home is stopped by another man wearing a mask. What is happening?" To solve this puzzle they will have to shift gears from the obvious—that the man's home is the place where he lives. When I tell you that the context is a baseball game, it all makes sense. Here's another: "A man rode into town on Friday. He stayed three days and left on Friday. How could this be?" You will have to wait until the end of the chapter for the answer.

SELF-MONITORING requires stepping outside of yourself to take a look at what you're doing. Optimally, the self-monitoring controls should be on at all times, hovering in the background like an alarm system. Self-monitoring plays a role in almost every other executive function. Both response control and emotional control require stepping outside yourself to have a look at what is really going on. Effective problem solving requires the periodic review of a plan to assess how it's working. As discussed in chapter 2, self-awareness is just beginning to emerge in adolescence.

SUSTAINING ATTENTION AND CONCENTRATION. Attention is to the brain what breathing is to the body—we hardly notice it operating but could not survive without it. Even our lizard brain can pay attention. While many brain systems contribute to this basic but vital function, it is the prefrontal cortex that regulates it. We tend to think about the concept of attention in black and white: Either you have it or you don't. However, it is much more complicated than that. Someone must first direct attention to where it needs to go (initiate), keep it there for as long as is necessary (sustain), prevent it from moving to something else that might be more appealing (inhibit), and then, at the appropriate time, move it somewhere else (shift).

ORGANIZATION. Life is 90 percent maintenance, and thus requires a lot of organization. Organization is not actually one of the executive functions; rather, it's a product of them. Yet when parents and teachers hear about the executive functions they immediately jump here, because it is so central to academic success. Unfortunately, for many people cleaning out a notebook, closet, or room is boring and tedious. This is part of the reason that people with ADHD are often messy—for them boredom equals death.

Organization can be broken down into two categories, which parallel how the brain processes information: verbally and visually. Keeping track of your things is a visual-spatial task. *Where did I put this? Where did I see it last? Where should it go?* Time management involves the verbal half of our brains (for most people, the left hemisphere). This is because verbal information is sequential: When you read a word you start at the left and move to the right. By the way, I have an excellent method to estimate how long household jobs will take—I determine how much time to set aside, and then add on three hours.

SELF-TALK. We talk to ourselves all day long. This private speech is crucial to many aspects of executive functioning. For example, we often converse with ourselves when we reflect on an event or situation before taking action (working memory and self-monitoring). We use self-talk to cue ourselves to turn off the computer and start doing the laundry, or to pick up the dry cleaning on the way home from work. Remember, the operative word here is *self*. It's not the same if you tell your son to pick up after himself, clean his room, or do his homework. But we'll get to that. Private speech plays a central role in self-regulation. (*Slow down.*

Stop and think!) Language is the best coping mechanism we have to deal with feelings.

The Organ of Civilization

So far we have been talking about the executive functions as existing solely within an individual, helping to regulate behavior in order to achieve a unique set of self-defined goals. However, executive functioning plays a vital role in the development of the species. Regulate the collective behaviors of a clan, tribe, or society toward a common objective, and achievements like the ancient wonder Machu Picchu or putting a man on the moon are possible. This is why Dr. Alexander Luria, the father of neuropsychology, has called the executive functions the "organ of civilization," and why Dr. Russell Barkley, one of the foremost researchers on attention deficit hyperactive disorder and executive functions, wrote that they allow us to be "social animals." In evolutionary terms, the prefrontal cortex has given us a tremendous advantage over other species—we can plan ahead, respond more flexibly to changes in our environment, and simulate possible outcomes in our head. Without the prefrontal cortex we would still be swinging from vines or, worse, hanging out in a swamp instead of at TGI Friday's®.

This cultural component plays an important role in an opt-out's lack of motivation. It is not just that the opt-out has executive functioning deficits, or that his prefrontal cortex is slower to develop. He also has difficulty buying in to the collective goals set by our society. This leads straight into the work of Dr. Howard Gardner.

HILL, SKILL, AND WILL. You may have heard of Dr. Gardner's theory of "multiple intelligence," as it's had a big impact on education. If not, check out the list of recommended readings at the end of the book. Gardner believes that there are eight kinds of intelligence—meaning there is no *one* way to be smart—and that everyone can make a contribution to our society.

According to Dr. Gardner, the executive functions emerge from "intrapersonal intelligence"—how well you know yourself. This involves self-awareness, introspection, and an ability to predict your reaction to new situations. He breaks executive functions down into three parts: (1) *Hills* are goals—who a person wants to be and where he wants to go in life; (2) *skills* are the abilities and techniques necessary to meet those goals; and (3) *will* is the effort and motivation that connects hills to skills. These components operate differently across one's life span. During childhood and adolescence, a period Gardner refers to as the apprentice stage, children are taught information and skills that will be useful in society. He writes, "Skill development predominates as children master the knowledge and know-how their societies and cultures require for them to become full participants."

This process of socialization trains children to understand their place in culture: which feelings are okay to express and which ones are personal; which behaviors are appropriate and how to perceive the actions of others. To a large extent, culture serves as a regulatory and control system—one that prepares its young to make it on their own one day.

Consider the difference in expectations placed on children in a nomadic herding tribe and those of kids in a typical American suburb. A nomad child must learn the ins and outs of animal husbandry and is expected to someday take his or her place as an adult member of the tribe. A child raised in Samesville, USA, must master a set of subjects we deem necessary to be educated (reading, writing, and math) in order that he can one day leave home and move anywhere that provides him the best economic opportunity.

Will, during the apprentice stage, falls largely on external enforcers like parents (*brush your teeth*; *write your grandmother a thank-you note!*) and teachers (*do this math worksheet tonight*; *the paper is due a week from Friday*). Hopefully, as children grow they begin to adopt the values they have been taught, and to internalize the goals set for them. When this happens, *will* becomes intrinsic. It emanates from within the individual.

However, this doesn't always happen. I often see unmotivated teens rebuff the goals society has set for them. They will refuse to learn algebra, master a five-paragraph essay, or aim for admission to a "good" college. Think back to the opening paragraph of chapter 1, where I mention the typical opt-out's feelings about school: "The teachers are stupid, the curriculum is irrelevant, math is just moving numbers around, and English is just moving words around. No one ever needs to know geometry, and Shakespeare is an absolute waste of time."

Hopefully, apprentices will advance to become masters—the destination stage in Gardner's theory. To become a master, an individual must have internalized his culture's values and acquired the necessary skills and knowledge to develop personally meaningful goals. These are the thinkers and innovators of society, the ones "who do not limit themselves to climbing hills offered by their culture, but instead scale hills that may not have existed before." The transition from apprentice to master usually occurs between ages twenty-five and thirty, but not everyone makes it to this stage. Many people function very well in jobs where their employer defines the goals.

Focus on the opt-out

Gardner's theory sheds a whole new light on the opt-out. The goals we expect young people to achieve are not their goals—they are the ones we believe will help them answer the questions *Who am I?* and *What will I become?* The problem is that your son doesn't buy in to these goals, at least not on the surface. And because his executive functions are undeveloped, he lacks the foresight to see the hole he is digging for himself. Clearly he needs some help. However, because teens are so determined to establish their own independence, the last thing they want is a parent holding their hand. Self-regulation is the cornerstone of true independence, and while all adolescents continue to need structure and support, the opt-out needs even more. And yet he is the one who fights it the most.

The early parenting sage Haim Ginott said it well when he described a teen as "like a person needing a loan but wishing he was financially independent." To help your son, you need to respect his autonomy. You need an approach that hovers in the background, a way to provide support without him even knowing you are doing it. In the world of psychology, this is called scaffolding.

Scaffolding

As you've surely noticed, children aren't very good at controlling themselves and thinking ahead. They still need adult guidance to wash behind their ears, turn off the television every once in a while, and raise a hand in class before talking. High school students may think they are all grown up, but they, too, need limits and reminders because, until the executive functions are fully established, adults must play the role of an external prefrontal cortex. Scaffolding is something parents do instinctively when their children are small—adding support until their kids are able to do something independently. Holding hands to cross a street, cutting food so kids can feed themselves, letting them read the words they can . . . and helping them sound out the ones they can't. Intuitively, you've been guiding and encouraging your son to do those things that are just beyond his capabilities. In essence, scaffolding is what happens when a parent or teacher helps a child master a skill or ability that the child is *almost* able to do.

Scaffolding dovetails the progression of human development. Abilities and skills do not simply surface overnight; they emerge gradually. Before they do, however, there is a phase of readiness called the Zone of Proximal Development, or ZPD. I realize these initials sound like the name of a fraternity, but this zone is more like the runway a plane must travel in order to pick up enough speed to take off. In reality, as the brain's circuitry develops, abilities start to emerge but are not yet stable—it's the wobbling you see just before a toddler walks, or the stumbling and sounding-out a new reader does before achieving fluency. The ZPD is the area between what a child or teen can do independently, and what he is able to manage with some assistance.

Scaffolding is very different from overparenting. Scaffolding supports your son's executive functions; overparenting takes control of them. To make sure you stay on the right side of the ZPD, follow a rule outlined in chapter 1: Less is more. By solving *less* of his problems and giving him *more* independence to solve them himself, you will support his executive functions. If you talk *less* and listen *more*, your son will begin to discover his feelings (emotional control) through self-awareness. If you talk *less* about your values and *more* about his, he will begin to develop his own goals. If you control *less* and structure *more*, your son will learn better time management and self-regulation.

Tools to Support Executive Functioning

WHAT IS YOUR PLAN?

Using scaffolding as a base, let's look at some other ways to help your son become better at planning, self-monitoring, and developing effective strategies. Think of your role not as a drill sergeant, teacher, or coach but rather as a facilitator who will guide your son to better problem solving. Don't drown him in reminders and requests. Instead, make him tired of hearing you ask, "What is your plan?" "Mom, I want to go camping this weekend with Jimmy and Devon." "Interesting, what is your plan?" "Mom, I got a C− on my math test, but the class average was a B−, so I didn't do so bad." "Great, what is your plan for bringing up your grade?" This is not some magic way to get your son to do what you want him to do—most of the time he will answer, "I don't know." But it is a way of reinforcing the idea that most good things that happen in life require a plan. It also reinforces the idea that your son is capable of devising and implementing a solution. This approach creates teachable moments out of things that you might otherwise be interpreted as nagging.

Remember, your son does not buy in to all of the goals society has set for him. He will be more cooperative when the goal is his ("I want to see the new superhero movie this week") than when it is yours ("You need to improve your grades"). However, when he tells you he has no plan to pass his chemistry test next week, you can reply, "Well, you will probably like the plan I come up with a lot less than one you come up with, so give it some thought." Likewise, you will usually need to set some parameters to his plan ("Will her parents be home?" "Jimmy just got his license yesterday and you want to drive to the mountains this weekend?"). That is when you take off the facilitator cap and put your parenting one back on.

How to Plan a Plan
Provide scaffolding by doing the following:

- Know your son's limits—what he can do independently and what he needs assistance with. This will help you to manage your own expectations.
- Get your son's interest by letting him know what's in it for him to make a plan. (This might include holding him accountable, which will be discussed in chapter 10.)
- Manage your son's frustration by keeping tasks simple and postponing a conversation when he gets overwhelmed.
- Let him do the work, but ask questions to lead him along or point out things that might help.
- Regulate your assistance, giving your son only enough to keep him going.

Here are the steps to constructing a solid plan:

- Define the goal or problem that needs to be solved.
- Identify the information needed to accomplish the goal or solve the problem (and where that information can be found).
- Determine if any help is needed to solve the problem or achieve the goal.
- Determine how long it will take (time management).
- Establish an order for the steps needed to achieve the goal/solve the problem. Note: This step is crucial, as it teaches your son to make a list. It's fine if he dictates and you write it down on the back of an envelope. Make the process informal and easily accessible (organization and time management).
- Identify useful strategies for achieving the goal/solving the problem. (See the following table.)

- Midway check-in: Somewhere along the way check in to see if things are going according to plan (reinforces self-monitoring).
- Assess the outcome (self-monitoring).

The following is a table that lists the steps and questions to ask. This chart uses two situations that require a plan: improving your son's chemistry grade and going camping with friends.

PLAN A PLAN

STEP	ASK	CHEMISTRY TEST	CAMPING WITH FRIENDS
State the problem/goal	What do you want to accomplish?	Raise grade on next test to a B.	Go camping with friends.
Identify information	What information do you need to achieve this goal/ solve this problem?	When is the test? What will be covered? Are your notes complete? Do you understand the material?	Who is going? Where will you go? How will you get there? Who will chaperone?
Get help	Do you need any help to achieve this goal/accomplish this problem?	Do you need to meet with a tutor or your teacher, or get help from Mom or Dad? Whose notes can you photocopy?	Who's been camping before and knows how to set up a tent, cook, and bear-proof your food? Who knows the best spots around?
Assess time	Let's take a look at the calendar and get a sense of the time frame.	How many hours a day do you think you need to put in?	When will you get the gear together and pack up? How far is the campground?

STEP	ASK	CHEMISTRY TEST	CAMPING WITH FRIENDS
Stepwise approach	Let's make a list of all the steps, in the order that you need to complete them. You talk, I will write.	1. Review my notes to see if they are complete. 2. Skim the chapter to see if I understand the concepts. 3. Schedule time to get extra help with my teacher. 4. Plan to study 30 minutes a day.	1. See who can come and who can chaperone. 2. Delegate responsibilities. 3. Make a list of the meals and ingredients. 4. Make a list of all the supplies and where you can get them. 5. Get info on the campground—directions, hours, etc.
Identify strategies	What study skills will you use? How will you manage all of this information?	Do you need flash cards? Will you review someone else's notes? Is there a test review sheet? Do you want us to quiz you?	Maybe you should get a notebook or make a spreadsheet to keep track of all this information. How about delegating the different jobs—each person can be responsible for planning and implementing one thing (cooking, supplies, etc.)?
Midway check-in	How will you know you are on track, will finish on time, did not leave anything to the last minute?	Maybe on Sunday you should take a step back and see if you feel you are on track, know as much as you thought you did, see if there is anything else to do.	Maybe a week before you go, you should have a meeting on Skype with everyone to assess your progress and see if there are any roadblocks.

STEP	ASK	CHEMISTRY TEST	CAMPING WITH FRIENDS
Assess outcome	So how did it go? What did you learn from this? What would you do differently?	What grade did you get? Did you meet your goal? If so, what worked? If not, what do you need to do differently?	How was the trip? Did you remember to bring everything? What advice would you give some-one else who is planning this kind of trip?

THINK STRATEGICALLY. Strategies are the products of executive functions. A strategy is like a mini plan or process that helps us approach tasks more efficiently. For instance, hanging up keys is a strategy many people use every day so as not to lose them—they just don't think to call it that. Teachers use learning strategies all the time. Maybe you know of this one: COPS (Capitalization, Organization, Punctuation, Spelling). Children using COPS write it on the top of their papers to help with proofreading.

Teach a child a strategy and he will be efficient for a day; teach a child to make up his own strategies, and he will be efficient for a lifetime. (Okay, maybe that doesn't roll off the tongue quite as nimbly as the fish line, but you see what I'm getting at.) People with ADHD have chaotic lives because they don't see the messes they create, such as overdrawn checking accounts or lost belongings. With patients, I discuss the importance of recognizing a mess or a repeated pattern of things gone awry. Once we identify these messes, we talk about strategies for cleaning them up. It looks something like this:

- Repeatedly lose a cell phone or wallet? Do a "lump check" every time you enter or leave a room.
- Can't find your checkbook because you thought storing it in the glove compartment was a good idea when the DMV was closed? ("It will be there tomorrow when I go back to

the DMV," you may have told yourself). Don't think, *This is a clever place to* put *something.* Rather, ask yourself, *Is this a clever place to* find *something?*

Helping your son develop his own strategies is an excellent way to scaffold executive functions. It requires thinking ahead and self-monitoring, and it can effectively compensate for working memory lapses (like forgetting where the checkbook is) and disorganization. A strategy can be a rule (hang up your keys) or a process (using an acronym). So when you see your son make a mess (both figuratively and literally), tell him he needs to think strategically. See what he comes up with on his own, and if he can't propose anything constructive, give him a few suggestions; let him figure out what works best. Asking "What is your strategy?" is more effective than nagging and—bonus!—your son will find it less aggravating.

Do you recall the Camster from chapter 1? He was the prototype Mr. Popular. One of the ways I helped Cam was to challenge him to do his homework every night for a month to see if it helped his grades. Cam was up for the challenge, but needed a few strategies. He rejected all of mine (like, *Do your homework in the kitchen as soon as you get home from school*). Instead he decided to do something uniquely Cam. He knew that at his school the top rankings were disproportionately held by Asian students, so he Googled "Asian study habits." He rejected one, "wear warm clothes," but "listening to classical music" appealed to him. This was because Cam hates classical music, so having it on motivated him even more to get his work done. Only Cam. But it worked.

MANTRAS. A mantra is something you say to yourself repeatedly to aid in mediation. What, you may be wondering, does this have to do with executive functions? Mantras are a lot like self-talk. Dr. Mary Solanto, a psychologist who has used cognitive behavioral therapy to help adults with ADHD, discovered a strategy that your teen can use. She found that saying specific slogans over and over scaffolds self-talk. Mantras can also be used as cues to help your son become more organized and complete tasks.

Below are a couple of my favorite mantras you may want to try out:

"What's the plan, Stan?"
"Think strategically."

And here are some more that came out of Dr. Solanto's research:

"If it's not in the planner, it doesn't exist."
"If you're having trouble getting started, then the first step is too big."
"Do all things in order of priority."
"Getting started is the hardest part."
"A place for everything, and everything in its place."
"Out of sight, out of mind."
"What you don't do today won't go away, it will just be that much harder tomorrow."

Based on feedback and discussion with the teens themselves, Dr. Solanto has devised a couple of teen-friendly mantras:

"Just shut up and do it and they'll get off your back."
"If you don't do it now, you're going to get screwed."

You may also want to invent mantras of your own. Whatever does the trick! Just repeat them often, and maybe even put one on a sign and hang it up on your fridge.

STRATEGIES AND TECHNIQUES. The following strategies fall into the category of "your teen may not be willing to do these." A cumbersome name, for sure, but it really gets to the point. Regardless, these strategies are enormously helpful. And when they're combined with other approaches outlined later in this book, your son will be more game:

- TAKE TWENTY-FIVE. Break down work into twenty-five-minute segments—twenty minutes of work followed by a five-minute break. This is known as a Pomodoro®. The Pomodoro Technique® was named after the tomato-shaped kitchen timer that was ubiquitous in pre-digital American homes (*pomodoro* means "tomato" in Italian). During the five-minute break, only one thing can be done (say, go to the bathroom or get a snack). After three or four Pomodoros, a fifteen-minute break is earned. There are many Pomodoro apps available for computers and smartphones. Check out the website pomodorotechnique.com to learn more.
- THE CIRCLE TECHNIQUE. During a twenty-minute work period use the circle technique to track distractions. Draw a circle and, while working, make a mark in it every time you get distracted or feel the urge to drift. Take a moment to ponder why, and then return to work. At the end of a Pomodoro, count the marks. We will build on this method later when we discuss anxiety.
- PROCRASTINATE THE DISTRACTION. Either next to the circle or on another sheet of paper, write down the activity trying to lure you away from homework (for example, check Instagram, return a text, or play a video game). Then, if you still feel the itch, indulge yourself at the next break.
- PLAN FORWARD. Many coaches and tutors suggest using a homework planner that includes an option for teens to esti-mate the time each assignment will take, as well as a record

of how long it really took. This function helps teens plan their study schedules, and it also improves their abilities to estimate. Below is my version (you can find a blank copy in the appendix on page 231).

HOMEWORK PREDICTOR

TIME PREDICTOR			DIFFICULTY PREDICTOR	
Assignment	How long do you estimate this assignment will take?	How long did it actually take?	Predict how hard this assignment will be on a scale of 1 (easy) to 5 (difficult).	How hard did you actually find it (using the same scale)?
Define vocab words	20 minutes	35 minutes	4	2

- WORK BACKWARD. For long-term assignments, using either a list or a grid format, write down each step of a long-term assignment. Write down the due date next to the last step ("hand it in"). From there, work backward, writing due dates next to each item until you reach today's date (item 1). Here is an example:

WORKING BACKWARD—HISTORY PAPER:

1. Select topic.	(Today's Date:_____)
2. Formulate hypothesis.	(Due Date:_____)
3. Collect resources (books, articles, websites).	(Due Date:_____)
4. Conduct research.	(Due Date:_____)
5. Make outline.	(Due Date:_____)
6. Write first paragraph.	(Due Date:_____)
7. Write X paragraphs (could be several, depending on the length of the paper).	(Due Date:_____)
8. Write conclusion.	(Due Date:_____)
9. Proofread.	(Due Date:_____)
10. Make revisions.	(Due Date:_____)
11. Hand it in.	(Due Date:_____)

Marydee Sklar, who developed the Sklar Process, advocates making this list more visual by putting it into a grid.

PLANNING BACKWARD

Select Topic Date:	Formulate Hypothesis Date:	Collect Resources Date:	Conduct Research Date:
Make Outline Date:	Write First Paragraph Date:	Write Body Paragraphs Date:	Write Body Paragraphs Date:
Write Conclusion Date:	Proofread Date:	Revise Date:	HAND IT IN! Date:

The next step is to transfer these steps to a calendar, starting from the day the project is due and working backward. Some steps may need several days.

- OUTLINE. There are several things teens never do: pick up their socks, date their notes, paginate their papers, and write an outline. Minus the socks, these essential aspects of writing are made much easier with a software program called Inspiration®. I used it to write this book. Inspiration allows the user to create a visual web, transfer it into a linear outline, and transfer that into a word-processing document. Check it out at inspiration.com.

Procrastination

Procrastination is the ultimate form of avoidance because it works so well. It is caused by anxiety, which is easily eliminated by doing something more pleasurable, like playing a video game.

But anxiety about what? Procrastination expert Dr. Neil Fiore suggests that procrastination is not the problem; instead, it is an attempt to resolve a number of underlying issues, including:

- fear of failure
- perfectionism
- boredom
- being overwhelmed

Recently, Canadian researchers, including Dr. Timothy Pychyl and Dr. Piers Steel, have hypothesized two more traits that distinguish people who procrastinate from those who don't: impulsivity and a poorly defined vision of themselves in the future. While many are motivated by a small jolt of anxiety, an English psychologist, Dr. Fuschia Sirois, has another idea about procrastinators: She believes they are less connected to their future selves than are those whose concrete and personal vision of their future selves keeps them on track.

Many of the strategies (especially planning backward) can help your son from becoming overwhelmed. Breaking down a task into smaller components will also help him feel less afraid of failure, because smaller tasks are more manageable and less daunting. This is one reason why outlining is so important.

Procrastination, however, is also about something else: power. It is a way that the powerless can gain an advantage over the powerful. Labor unions have relied on this method—the work slowdown—for many years as a way of averting a strike. Your son, who at least on the surface sees his homework as irrelevant and meaningless, fights back against authority (the culture that defines his hill and skill) by reserving the right to work at his own pace. Dr. Fiore's words speak volumes here: "As a powerless victim you feel you cannot openly rebel because . . . that

would mean risking the probable consequences—anger and punishment . . . but by procrastinating, you temporarily, secretly
dethrone the authority and you can resist by dragging your feet
and giving a halfhearted effort." We will explore this dynamic in
the second half of this book. For now, though, here are a couple
of useful strategies to deal with procrastination.

1. *Do it or do nothing*: Pick a task, set the Pomodoro, and get
   to work. If your son has writer's block or is otherwise stuck,
   do nothing else. Even if his circle becomes completely filled
   in with all his "distraction marks," consider this part of the
   process. Have him take a five-minute break when the buzzer
   goes off and, if necessary, repeat. Eventually the faucet
   will open and the work will begin to flow. (Remember, you
   can offer this strategy to your son as a suggestion, not as a
   requirement.)
2. Give your son the following procrastination log to fill out. It
   will help him to not only track his work, but also to become
   aware of his anxiety and rationalizations.

PROCRASTINATION LOG

ASSIGNMENT	THOUGHTS ABOUT THE ASSIGNMENT	ACTION YOU TOOK	JUSTIFICATION FOR PROCRASTINATION	RESULT
Write English essay	I am not going to do well on it.	Took an Instagram, Facebook, or YouTube "break."	"It's not due until Thursday."	Put it off and stayed up till 2 a.m. Wednesday to get it done.
Math worksheet	I got this.	Completed assignment.	N/A	Got 100.

* The answer to the riddle: Friday was his horse.

5

Big Boys Don't Cry

I realized the other day that if I did not have friendships with women, I would never understand emotions or talk about them. Men are emotionally illiterate. All they can talk about is work, jokes, sports, and women.

—JOSH, TWENTY-THREE-YEAR-OLD GRADUATE STUDENT

My friends and I are a posse. We hang out in a bathroom at school that is out of the way, so no one comes in there. The group is closed to new members, and it gives me a sense of security. We never talk about real things, unless it's just me and my best friend. The posse usually makes fun of other people, or we tease each other. We talk about girls, but never anything personal, like who someone might really like.

—MIKE, AGE SIXTEEN

Which boys have the most status? The ones who have the most money to burn, the ones who have a good sense of humor and can keep the conversation going, and the ones who are either the best athletes or the ones who know the most about sports. For girls, it's all about looks.

—JAKE, AGE FIFTEEN

I have counseled boys in therapy for over twenty-five years. Prior to that, starting at age sixteen, I was a camp counselor and then a child-care worker. And before that I was a boy. So, I know a little bit about them. Put a group of males together, and their physicality, exuberance, and energy are difficult to contain. Boys can be wonderfully rambunctious and mischievous. Often the only way to rein one in is to tire him out. Though they are competitive and aggressive, there is also simplicity to their relationships. Tempers flare quickly, but boys do not stay angry for long; they respond to an insult by throwing back a clever retort or even a punch, and the conflict is soon forgotten. Girls' squabbles, on the other hand, take days to resolve through an indirect web of ever-changing alliances. When I was a camp counselor, the girls' staff spent much of their time mending hurt feelings, while on the boys' side we tended to bruises, bloody noses, and broken bones.

As simple as a boy's life can be, growing into manhood is no small challenge. In his *Time* magazine cover story, "The Myth About Boys," David Von Drehle writes, "The cultivation of boys has been an obsession for thousands of years." He invokes Socrates, who asked, "How shall we find a gentle nature which also has a great spirit?"

In order to understand the opt-out phenomenon, you have to appreciate how hard it is to become a man. Unlike girls, whose femininity is rarely called into question, teenage boys must constantly prove their masculinity. A boy's manhood is continually tested, and unlike his school exams these are tests he cares deeply about passing.

Anything but Feminine

Boys love to compete, especially to prove who is the toughest. Those spirited ten-year-old boys I encountered as a camp counselor were forever trying to best one another—who was the fastest, who was the funniest, who could fart the loudest or burp the alphabet. They were constantly teasing each other and putting one another down. The key was to show no pain, hide any hurt feelings, recover with a quick comeback, and move on. There was, however, one put-down that was feared above all others: "faggot."

Even today, when homosexuality is more socially accepted than ever before, the word "gay" is still thrown around the halls and locker rooms of middle and high schools to signify weakness, the ultimate male put-down. No one said managing adolescence is easy for a girl—she may be called a poser, ho, slut, or stuck-up—but chances are good that her womanhood will likely never be called into question. Boys, on the other hand, "not only feel the pressure to appear masculine," according to the best-selling book *Raising Cain: Protecting the Emotional Life of Boys* by Dan Kindlon and Michael Thompson, "but they feel that, in doing so, they must be clearly *not* feminine . . . and so they consciously and deliberately attack in others and in themselves traits that might possibly be defined as feminine. This includes tenderness, empathy, compassion, and any show of emotional vulnerability." A boy's credo is Anything but Feminine (ABF).

Boys definitely want girls' attention, but it is other boys they look to for validation of their masculinity. Your son's idea of masculinity is defined by a group of boys his age who are as clueless as he is about what it means to be a man. Teenage boys, insecure about who they are and how to fit in, look up to peers who seem to have it figured out, like the best athletes or the cool dudes. And because it so dangerous to be weak, boys form a rigid, exaggerated male ideal, one reinforced by our culture and modeled after the invulnerable and invincible: professional athletes, rap singers, superheroes, action movie stars, and even video game warriors. To be masculine is to walk a tightrope, and any small step off the narrow path is perilous. A patient in his early twenties recalled, as a teen, wanting to be like his anime hero from a popular Japanese cartoon: "He made the girls drool. He was stoic, and had a mysterious past. That is what I tried to be, a dark, ironic anti-hero." Another patient, fifteen years old, described his own struggle this way: "Masculinity provides a safety net for someone who does not know who they are. It is okay to try on different shoes. If you really do not know who you are, it is better to try to be like someone else than to be someone lost."

Teenage boys form a boy credo whose primary tenet is ABF. Much of the homophobia expressed when boys call each other "faggot" is not even about being gay—it's about boys' fear that other boys will see them as feminine. The unspoken oath of boyhood is that you will not be "a sissy, nerd, wimp, or wuss."

BIG BOYS DON'T CRY

The boy code training starts early. Starting at around four years old, boys are told, "Big boys don't cry." And this is just the beginning. Beyond "faggot" and "gay," boys are constantly told by their friends, coaches, and even fathers not to be "a pussy" or a "little girl." Then there are the admonitions to be more masculine: "grow a pair," "man up," and "act like a man." In our sports-crazed culture, the sideline ethos is to shake off any injury and get back in the game. It's no wonder that concussions have risen to epidemic proportions in sports at every level.

Masculinity is measured in numbers: how tall you are, how fast you can run. As boys grow older, this changes to how many girls you get into the sack, and how much money you make. Boys and men are forever comparing themselves to one another. This leads to endless teasing, mostly done in fun, about any quirky behavior or physical characteristic. Nicknames abound in the world of boys: A guy with pimples is known to his friends as "pizza face," a pale-skinned teen is called Casper (the friendly ghost) by his fraternity brothers, and a football player's nickname "Thunder" (short for "Thunder Thighs") is used even by his teachers and coaches (but not his mother, who still calls him William). However, this measuring up has a dark side. In order to fit in, boys must play a role, and to do that they must sacrifice their authenticity.

THE STOIC HERO

When academics write about masculinity they speak in terms of a performance. James Mahalik's research has identified several scripts that men follow: "strong and silent," "tough guy," "the playboy," and "the true competitor." A boy's only option is to play the role of the stoic hero, to never complain or show pain, and to always remain steadfast and confident. A stoic is tough and capable, and he believes that action speaks louder than words. In describing his father's stoicism, author Jeffery Marx wrote: "Highs and lows were for a weatherman reporting the temperature; my dad's emotional thermometer was generally stuck somewhere in the moderate middle. I always knew that he had strong beliefs because he showed them through his actions, never wavering in his commitments to family, always doing the right thing, and especially treating other people well. But actually talk about his feelings and emotions—express them in words? No. That was a foreign concept for my dad."

Since dependency and neediness are off limits, men face a DO NOT ENTER sign when they approach intimate connections. An adolescent boy's relationship with his mother is particularly threatening because she is the person whom, up until recently, he relied upon most.

MAMA'S BOY

If "faggot" tops the list of emasculating insults, "mama's boy" runs a close second. The female counterpart to "mama's boy" is "daddy's girl," which is hardly a put-down. This is because, in order for a boy to become a man, he has to separate from his mother in a way that girls do not. As infants and toddlers, both boys and girls both want to be like their "mommy." It's okay for little boys to play with dolls or a toy kitchen—up to a point. At about the same time boys are told to hold back the tears (around age four), they are also encouraged to cut the apron strings. The sociologist Nancy Chodorow suggests that, because a boy's first attachment is to his mother, in order to become a man he must eventually renounce this connection. This is where ABF originates—masculinity is defined from the start in negative terms: not being like mom.

While boys are discouraged from being too close to their mothers, girls never have to fully separate. As the old adage goes, "A son is a son till he gets a wife, but a daughter's a daughter all of her life." Girls don't have to choose. They can remain dependent on their parents (though certainly giving them hell during the teenage years), yet still feel independent. A boy, on the other hand, feels ashamed of his desire for approval and dependency because it makes him feel too needy and is therefore unacceptable. So he keeps his emotional distance, retreats into his room, and, when necessary, asserts his independence by opposition and fighting. This quest for masculinity makes a teenage boy's journey over the bridge of ambivalence even more complicated. Being dependent results in the double whammy of being both a child and also being feminine.

THE ALPHA MALE

Making intimacy off limits has repercussions for male friendships. Boys view relationships as hierarchical. Forever jockeying for a position of power, they must always appear knowledgeable. Girls, in comparison, live in a social world of constantly shifting rivalries and alliances, and they derive status from whom they know. For boys it's not who, but *what*, you know . . . and what you can do.

The boy who can hit a ball out of the park or is the first to best the newest version of Call of Duty® is the one who will earn the respect of his peers. Listen to a group of men discuss last night's basketball game. On the surface it sounds as though they are just talking sports, but lurking just below is a competition about who knows more. Middle and high school boys brag mainly about things like a sports achievement or a weekend hookup, but never about getting the lead in the school play or scoring a violin solo for the spring concert. As we will explore in the next chapter, masculinity goes hand in hand with athleticism but never comes from making the honor roll.

Research has shown that because boys do not like to talk about themselves the way that girls do, they tend to hang out around a specific activity. I know that during biking season I may talk to my riding buddies for hours, but I rarely see them when my bike is put down for the winter. Deborah Tannen, a linguist who focuses on gender differences, has very interesting things to say about how differently men and women relate. For example, in studying what children and teens do when asked to talk about a serious subject, she found that sixth-grade girls had no difficulty discussing feelings and friendship. As you might expect, their male counterparts could not sit still, and though they rambled from topic to topic, the subject of "feelings and friendship" rarely came up. By tenth grade, the girls' growing comfort with intimacy was apparent in how they pulled their chairs close together and made eye contact when talking. The boys may as well have been seated in church pews—they sat parallel to one another, eyes focused dead ahead. Surprisingly, from this detached, shoulder-to-shoulder posture, the boys were able to open up.

Generally, boys are able to form close friendships until they are young teens. But sadly, as they age, males tend to become more distrustful of their peers, leaving them feeling isolated and alone.

Perhaps, at some time in our primordial past, the instinct to mate forced men to see one another as competitors. I suspect, however, that the tendency of men to move away from one another has more to do with a qualification I hear over and over when teenage patients describe their close male friends: "no homo." Can you imagine a woman, referring to her girlfriend, adding a qualifier like "She's not my lesbian lover, just a friend"? Ridiculous.

Feelings, a No-Man's-Land

Without any safe way to understand or express their feelings, boys are left with only two possibilities. The first is to withdraw, which may be the only way your son knows to deal with his feelings of self-doubt, inadequacy, and fear. The second, less desirable, way is to act out feelings by fighting, being oppositional, or engaging in delinquent activities. Anger is the only feeling that boys and men can safely express; it's easier for them to get mad than sad.

Men use a triad of psychological defenses to shut down their feelings: avoidance, compartmentalization, and denial. As a parent of an opt-out, you know all about avoidance. It's like a magic wand your son waves across anything that makes him feel anxious. Then—poof!—it's gone: no more history paper, no more anxiety. Anxiety itself is not a feeling, it's a signal of impending danger, real or imagined. In this case, the danger is becoming a failure.

Procrastination is just avoidance by another name. If your son were Pinocchio, he'd have a very long nose because avoidance is predicated on a series of small lies he tells himself: "I will do it in five minutes" or "This will be easy." And then there are the ones he tells you, like "I will [take out the trash, wash the dishes, clean my room, do my homework . . .] later."

Compartmentalization is a way of quarantining feelings that

accompany any difficult situation (for instance, a marital spat over breakfast) in order to function at work, school, or anywhere else. This coping strategy is summed up by the phrase "Out of sight, out of mind." Feelings surrounding emotional events are packed up and stored away like Christmas ornaments in January. One patient, struggling with cancer, put it this way: "I visualize a series of boxes in my head and I keep them locked up. I open them up in therapy but, sometimes, not even there."

The danger is that these feelings can be pushed out altogether, which is the definition of denial. Denial requires rewriting history— "I never said that"; "I don't have a drinking problem"; "My grades are absolutely fine"—often with grievous consequences.

Behind their superhero capes and underneath their helmets and shoulder pads, however, boys do have feelings. And these feelings can get hurt. The toughness and detachment boys display are carefully honed to mask pain and vulnerability. Teenage boys do feel needy, just as they long for love and acceptance. But they do not have the words to describe these emotions, nor the insight to understand them. For many men, sexual intimacy is the only kind of closeness they can tolerate. Only in the bedroom can they experience vulnerability and dependency, which they do under the guise of satisfying their libido. When a man says, "I have needs," he thinks he is referring to one organ and doesn't realize he also means another: his heart. Today's hookup culture offers a detached sexuality that does not require any emotional intimacy. This type of sexuality is reinforced by all the pornography your son is watching. I have seen many boys confused by frequent hookups with an "FWB" (Friend with Benefits). Unsure what to do or how to feel—or worried that they have landed themselves in a relationship—they just "ghost" the girl: They stop talking to her and move on.

Behind the Mask

In order to survive, men live behind what William Pollock, author of *Real Boys*, one of the first books about boys, calls the "mask of masculine bravado." This mask allows boys and men to "cut themselves off from any feelings that society teaches them are unacceptable" by hiding their true, genuine selves. This mask also affords a man the only protection he knows against one of the most complicated emotions: shame.

When it comes to understanding shame, I turn to the work of Brené Brown. If you haven't already done so, check out her TED Talks "Listening to Shame" and "The Power of Vulnerability." Brown points out the difference between shame and guilt: Guilt means you did something wrong; shame means that you are wrong—the feeling that your thoughts or actions will force others to reject or even banish you, and that you are unworthy of human connection. Hester Prynne's shame was made public by the scarlet A she was forced to wear. In Leviticus, God provides a scapegoat for this difficult emotion, upon which the Jews could unload their shame every year and banish it to the wilderness.

Brown's research demonstrates that men and women have different triggers for shame. For men, shame is elicited by a direct hit across the bow of masculinity. For boys, particularly male teens, there are many missiles to duck, such as being homesick; being picked on or, worse, picked last; getting beat up; giving up; being scared off, too small, or too prudish; striking out; or breaking down.

Women, on the other hand, feel shame when they let someone down. Women are trained to be all things to all people, to meet everyone's needs, and to do so looking like they just stepped off the cover of *Vogue* or *Cosmo*. Because women are primed to be caregivers, motherhood is a battleground for shame. Much of their self-worth rests on the shoulders of their children's happiness. Fathers, of course, are equally invested in the well-being of their offspring, but their self-esteem tends to be offset by career success. In either case, relying on parenting success to feel good about yourself puts you on a collision course with your opting-out son.

Focus on the Opt-Out: The Three C's

This discussion of feelings sheds new light on the struggle between you and your son. Greater clarity leads to more effective parenting and problem solving. You take your son's lack of motivation personally. It is *your* job to fix *his* problem. He, on the other hand, is in the throes of separation and casting his own identity. This process, as you may recall from chapter 2 (page 23), is fraught with ambivalence because he is trying to hide lingering dependency. So when you nag him to do his homework you are reminding him that he still needs you—that he cannot figure this school thing out on his own—and he loses face.

To add to this complexity, chances are that his school difficulties did not materialize overnight. When he needed help as a child, you were his hero. It was hard, frustrating work, but I'm guessing that, at the end of an exhausting day, you felt good about yourself as a parent because you were doing everything you could think of to help your son, and that he came to rely on this help to get through school.

Fast-forward to the present. Now your son's failure becomes your shame. So you continue your mission to rescue him, this time with even more vigor. However, your son, who deep down feels shamed by his own inability to succeed, no longer wants your help because it just reinforces the mortifying message that he is failing and cannot succeed without you.

In order to avoid these feelings, he either shuts down or tries to gain power by becoming hostile and attacking you. In any event, the more he rejects your best intentions, the worse you feel. Without realizing it, you and your son are caught up in a web of shame.

A young man I know named Cody recently told me what it was like to grow up in this web. Now twenty-three years old, he recalled struggling with dyslexia as a teenager, while awaiting a growth spurt that would catapult him to a height of six feet two inches. At the time, he wanted to hide his disability from the world:

"When I was a teenager, I did not want anyone to know I was dyslexic. I was ashamed of it. Those were hard years. I feel bad for how much grief I gave my mom. She was just trying to help me—and man did she try, but I wanted no part of it. I just wanted to be one of the guys. It would have been social suicide if they knew my mom had to help me read. Being cool meant never trying hard at anything. Now I know those guys I looked up to secretly worked their butts off. But then, I believed them when they said, 'Man, I wrote that paper in an hour and still got an A.' I just focused on sports and did my best not to let anyone know how anxious I was inside."

Cody, like all opt-outs, had to hide his feelings of inadequacy in order to maintain his masculine composure. For boys like him it comes down to three issues: competence, control, and connection. As you will see in part II, self-determined motivation arises from a sense of feeling competent, in control, and connected to others. These three C's are intrinsically linked to masculinity.

COMPETENCE. Because boys must avoid feeling incompetent at all costs, struggling in school presents a threat to their masculinity. As Cody pointed out, the cool kids make school look easy. It is okay to break into a sweat playing soccer, but never while writing a paper. If your son does not feel in control at school because he gets easily bored, reads slowly, or is disorganized, he will rationalize that school does not really matter, resulting in a loss of motivation and engagement. He would rather compromise his grades than his self-worth as a confident and capable man.

CONTROL. Your son must feel he is the captain of his own ship, so he will interpret your efforts to motivate him as a threat to his command. He'll fight back with opposition that will likely result in a power struggle. If your son doesn't feel in control of his abilities to study, complete assignments, and get good grades, he's likely to disengage from the whole process. No student with a learning disability, ADHD, or weak executive functions can feel in control at school. However, he can control how much or how little he cares about it.

CONNECTION. A teenager is like a caterpillar shedding his cocoon. This may sound lovely, until you realize you are the cocoon! Keep in mind that he's in the throes of separation and wants to break his connection to you. Staying connected to any teen, let alone an opt-out, is tricky. This book is all about finding the balance between giving space and setting limits. The following suggestions will start you on this path, while still supporting your son's masculinity:

1. STOP TAKING YOUR SON'S OPTING OUT PERSONALLY. Your success as a parent should not be linked to his success as a student. Basing self-worth on a teenage boy's achievement is a losing proposition for both parent and child. I'm not talking about a need for your son to perform well so that you can feel good about yourself—we will get to that in chapter 11. I'm referring to a feeling that it's your fault if he's not achieving right now. As mentioned earlier, you have done everything you could, and now it is time to step out of the way. Well, for the most part, but your son still needs limits and to be held accountable. That is subject of a later chapter as well (chapter 10).

2. STOP MAKING YOUR SON'S OPTING OUT PERSONAL. Calling him lazy only contributes to his shame. The same is true when you accuse him of not caring about his future or working up to his potential. These attacks on his character, whether you mean it or not, communicate that he's not worthy of your love. For this reason, a paradigm shift is crucial. Focus instead on his behavior, such as not planning well enough, or not being prepared for a test. However, make sure to heed tip 5 below.

3. STOP TELLING HIM HOW SMART HE IS. This is a dangerous message. As discussed in chapter 1 (and I'm repeating myself because it's so important), measuring and evaluating your son's performance makes your love appear conditional. Now consider that this also causes him shame.

4. DO NOT LECTURE YOUR SON ABOUT BAD GRADES OR HARP ON HIS PREVIOUS FAILURES. As frustrated as you might be, this approach will also bring your son shame and cause him to shut down further. There's a big difference between acknowledging a problem and making him feel terrible about it.

5. DON'T NAG. Watch television, go out with friends, put duct tape over your mouth if you have to, but resist the urge to badger your son: It will only backfire, because he'll feel emasculated. Deborah Tannen's research suggests that the root of women's nagging is actually altruistic. Because, in general, women derive self-worth and status from relationships, a woman might think, *If my husband asked me to do something, I would certainly do it—so he must want to fulfill my request. He just needs a reminder.* Men, on the other hand, never like to be told what to do because it makes them feel less in charge, and therefore less masculine.

6. TRY COACHING INSTEAD. Tell your son, "Eventually you will figure out how to do school," rather than "You just don't care about school, do you?" It's the same message; you are just detoxifying it by reframing a criticism as a belief in your son's ability to solve the problem on his own. You are also referencing a time in the future when he will have more control and feel more competent.

7. CHOOSE YOUR WORDS CAREFULLY. Tannen also discovered that, because women seek affiliation, they use conversation to develop relationships and show concern. They offer up supportive comments or ask follow-up questions about feelings. Boys hate this kind of thing. Generally speaking, too many words will cause your opt-out to tune out. Whether it's "fatherly advice" on how to solve a problem, a maternal expression of concern, or even a parental breakdown of frustration, directives, suggestions, and prompts, your son's sense of masculine pride will be challenged. Even though he badly needs to listen to everything you have to say, too much advice will only reinforce your "one-up position." This, in turn, will result in a standoff where he'll assert his power by opting out.

8. WHEN HE DOES WANT TO TALK, LISTEN VERY CAREFULLY. Later I will tell you a lot more about how to listen empathically (page 173), but for now here are some tips garnered from the research literature on gender difference:

- William Pollock points out that boys talk on their own "emotional schedules": "How was your day?" might only get a "Fine," but later your son might be ready to tell you what's on his mind. Granted, it might be just as your head hits the pillow, but with teenage boys you must take what you are given. Less is more applies here too. Think of talking with your son as a long conversation that's broken down into bite-sized pieces.

- Give him "the silent treatment." When men do finally open up (and this is true for women as well), the only thing they want is to be heard. They don't want advice. They don't want to hear about what you went through as a child. They just want to know that you understand what they are going through, and that you care about them. If they are opening up and allowing themselves to be vulnerable, the last thing you want to do is risk shaming them.

9. TEACH HIM THE *SKILL* OF ASKING FOR HELP. Teach your son that asking for help is a skill, one you had to learn in order to be successful. Tell him about someone who helped you with your career or in life, and then explain that the key to asking for help is to develop a relationship with the person you hope will help you before you need their assistance. With a relationship previously established, people are more likely to make themselves available and offer honest feedback.

10. IF YOUR SON NEEDS HELP, TRY TO FIND A MAN TO DO THE JOB. In some cases a student from a local college who is willing to come over, keep your son on task, and offer help when asked is more effective than a tutor or executive skills coach. Your son will be more cooperative because he'll feel less threatened. I run a program like this in my practice. Teens come after school and do their homework under the supervision of a young male teacher. His primary job is to develop a relationship with them and keep them focused.

11. HELP YOUR SON BECOME AN EXPERT IN SOMETHING, EVEN IF IT IS NOT SCHOOL-RELATED. While his screen time might need to be limited, don't trivialize his love of video games—it might be the only place that he truly feels competent. Encourage him to take up extracurricular activities that follow his interests. They might not be the ones that will earn him male status among his peers, but they will help him to feel competent and effective. Encourage him to get a job. Mowing lawns and packing groceries are great ways for high school students to feel independent and gain a sense of accomplishment. Here's a tip: College admissions readers view work on par with fancy internships or service trips to Costa Rica. The admissions director of a competitive orthopedic residency once told me that the best residents had played sports and worked during high school or college.

Shame is like venom that poisons one's sense of self-worth and belonging. The good news is that there's an antidote to this poison; the bad news is that most men won't try it. That is because the cure for shame puts men in a classic "damned if you do, damned if you don't" situation. The cure for shame, as Brown tells us, is to get it out in the open, to unlock the compartment it is stored in, take out whatever "unworthy" act or feeling is causing the trouble, and share it with someone you trust. However, this means being vulnerable, which, for men, only leads to more shame.

Myth Buster: Vulnerability is not a sign of weakness; it is an act of courage

Believe this—live it!—and you will have turned our culture's rigid definition of masculinity on its head. It takes a lot of backbone for anyone, but especially men, to admit they are uncertain, hurt, or scared. This major paradigm shift is best illustrated by a story from nature told by Carl Safina. Safina is an accomplished defender of the environment, who has won MacArthur, Pew, and Guggenheim fellowships, hosted the PBS series *Saving the Ocean*, and written several books, including *Beyond Words: What Animals Think and Feel*. You can learn more about him at CarlSafina.org. Safina's recent *New York Times* op-ed, "Tapping Your Inner Wolf," caught my attention because it turned our notion of the Alpha Wolf on its head. Safina describes a "superwolf" named 21, who was followed for years by Yellowstone National Park's Rick McIntyre. McIntyre wasn't raised by wolves, but spent much of his adult life around them. The wolf 21 earned the "superwolf" moniker because he never lost a fight and ferociously defended his family. However, at home, 21 was far from a dominating "leader of the pack." Rather, according to McIntyre, he exuded a quiet confidence and self-assurance, led by example, knew what was best for his pack, and was a calming influence. He was a gentle father who not only loved wrestling with the pups but actually pretended to lose.

The true alpha male, according to Safina and McIntyre, is not aggressive, because he does not need to be. Rather, he is emotionally secure, having already proved what needs to be proved. In other words, he does not need to defend his masculinity. And, in our world, there is room for more than one way of being masculine.

At the beginning of this chapter, I shared with you some boys' perspectives on being a man. Here, now, are some other voices, ones that offer a more enlightened view of masculinity in line with the real alpha wolf:

"Being comfortable in your own skin, being comfortable with who you are. That is my definition of being a man. Not a guy who is afraid to show his pain."

—NOAH, AGE TWENTY-FOUR, FORMER HIGH SCHOOL

AND COLLEGIATE HOCKEY PLAYER

"My definition of masculinity? I feel like it's evolving. Growing up I would have definitely said, 'You have to be big and strong. Don't cry. You have to be able to take the lead.' Those characteristics do not belong to masculinity. They could apply to females as well. I guess that definition of being strong has changed for me—it is not having big muscles; it is being able to cope with difficult situations and being willing to fail."

—CHAI, AGE THIRTY-FIVE, FORMER HIGH SCHOOL
FOOTBALL PLAYER, CURRENT TEACHER AND COACH

"I am a man's man with feelings."

—PHILLIP, AGE FORTY-NINE, INVESTMENT BANKER AND PILOT (THIS
STATEMENT WAS MADE AFTER BEING CHIDED BY A FRIEND THAT
HE WAS A "WOMAN'S MAN," BECAUSE HE HUNG OUT IN THE
KITCHEN WITH THE WIVES DURING A SUPER BOWL™ PARTY)

As a society we must stop making men conform to a notion of masculinity that is only defined by what it's not. The goal is not to "feminize" men, but to stop pushing boys toward an exaggerated and stereotypic ideal, an ideal that forces them to shut down any part of themselves that does not adhere to a narrow conception of manliness. Or, in the words of Ka'eo Vasconcellos, an award-winning teacher and football coach whom you will hear more about in the next chapter, "We need to stop beating the softness out of boys."

This reimagined masculinity defines strength not in terms of domination and physical aggression, but rather in terms of moral courage and self-control. We should take a page from the alpha wolf's playbook and incorporate qualities like tenderness, compassion, and cooperation into our concept of masculinity, while still allowing men to be fierce and competitive.

There must be room for a man to be both independent and dependent, both strong and weak. Perhaps with our society's growing acceptance of same-sex unions, bisexuality, and trans-gender citizens, straight men won't feel threatened and feel they have so much to prove.

The payoff, according to Kindlon and Thompson, is a big one: "Boys fortified by emotional awareness and empathy are less likely to inflict hurt on others and more resilient under the pressure of cruelty that comes their way." It requires fathers to model emotional openness and empathy without fearing they will make "pussies" of their sons. Mothers will have to engage their sons in a dialogue about what kind of men they hope to raise. They must also strike a balance between giving their boys the space to grow into independent men, and still remaining close.

Things to Think About

For Dads

- Think about your own definition of masculinity.
- What were the messages you got from your father? What was your relationship with him like?
- How do you handle your own feelings and frustration?
- When was the last time you were afraid? Did you tell anyone about it?
- Do you tell your son about the mistakes you made and how you dealt with them?
- Do you talk about yourself, really reveal something about yourself, not to teach your son a lesson but to give him the chance to really know you? In other words, model taking off the mask.
- Can you relate to your son on an emotional level, talk to him

about feelings? Or is it all about giving him advice and teaching him a lesson?

- Do you still give him a hug and tell him how much you love him?

FOR MOMS

- Do your actions encourage your son to be independent? Do you clean up after him, rescue him, and treat him like royalty?
- Do your words encourage your son to be independent, or is your first question, "What can I do for you?"
- Do you give him the space to become a man?
- At the same time, do you still talk to him about how to treat women? About feelings?
- Are you really prepared to accept greater vulnerability, even failure, from the men in your life? From your father, your husband, your son?

FOR BOTH PARENTS

- Do you hold your son accountable for his actions, or do you let him off the hook based on a boys-will-be-boys mentality?
- Do you encourage him to be open by refraining from lecturing or talking too much so you can listen to him talk? When he talks, do you respect his feelings and honor his opinions? (See chapter 10 for more on this subject.)
- Do you have confidence that he will figure things out; that eventually he will grow into a confident man who finds his place in the world, even though it does not seem possible right now?

Too Cool for School

Chai Reddy teaches at Honolulu's prestigious Punahou School. Back in 1979, when Chai was still in diapers, Punahou won the state basketball championship. You might have heard of their point guard that year, Barack Obama. Today Chai leads Punahou's International Center, is an admissions officer, and coaches football. The son of Indian immigrants, Chai grew up in Oklahoma, where he played football in high school. He earned a master's degree in the classics and has taught history, science, and math.

Just up the road from Punahou School sits Roosevelt High School. Although it serves a much less privileged student body, this public institution has also produced its share of illustrious alumni, including professional baseball player Michael Lum, a congressman, a chief justice of Hawaii, and pop singer Bruno Mars. Ka'eo Vasconcellos, a native Hawaiian, is one of Roosevelt's finest teachers. In fact, in 2012 the City of Honolulu named him teacher of the year. Ka'eo is a social studies teacher who also coaches football.

Both these men have given serious thought to boys and school. For instance, Ka'eo was so concerned about how many of Roosevelt's male students were dropping out before graduation that he returned to school himself to study the problem; his doctoral dissertation was titled "Hawaiian Male Adolescent Students' Perceptions of Masculinity." I encourage you to check out his TED Talk: "What Maketh a Man?"

Even at Punahou, where some students come from privileged backgrounds, Chai sees boys struggling. "It doesn't matter what you are teaching," he said of his days as a teacher, "it's going to be more challenging for a boy than it is for a girl in a traditional classroom. They do not have the frontal lobe development yet. It's the boys, not the girls who get into trouble." And as an admissions officer, Chai notices that girls are much stronger applicants than boys—they have better grades, are more articulate in interviews, and think more creatively.

Ka'eo understands why the boys he teaches act "too cool for school." "What's the incentive to learn," he wonders, "if you are called a fag? Girls don't say, 'He's hot because he is smart.' It's the abs, the muscles." He's also not surprised that boys hate to read; there is so little literature that is relevant and engaging for them to latch on to.

Tween and teenage boys prove their manliness on the field and in the locker room, not in the classroom. Doing well in school is for girls and nerds. In fact, boys who succeed academically are pressured to play it down. Being a good student is only cool if it comes naturally and without effort. When a popular boy gets an A on a test, he'll likely explain it away to his friends by saying, "I hardly studied"—even though he did. Some boys master the art of secretly doing well in school. But not the opt-out; he just doesn't try.

Chai and Ka'eo's concerns are well founded. Books such as *The War Against Boys* (Christina Hoff Sommers), *Boys Adrift* (Leonard Sax), and *The Trouble with Boys* (Peg Tyre) are testament to what has become known as "the boy crisis." In an article for *The*

New Republic, Richard Whitmire writes, "Given the demands of today's college curriculum, that means a lot of boys out there are falling short of being considered 'college material.' Which is why women now significantly outnumber men in college campuses . . . At some point in the early '80s, boys' relative academic records and aspirations took a downward turn. So far, no one has come up with a good explanation for this trend."

According to the Department of Education, which tracks the progress of America's students through a semiannual "report card," the gender gap is growing. With very few exceptions, girls have outpaced boys in both math and English since 1971, when the report card was first issued. A recent analysis of nearly 370 studies, encompassing over one million subjects, found that girls outperformed boys in every academic subject, including science. And this problem is worldwide.

Compared with boys, girls:

- Participate more in extracurricular activities (student government, honors societies, school newspapers, and debating clubs).
- Do more homework (as much as four times more by twelfth grade).
- Have higher college admission rates. Since 1994 there has been an 8 percent increase in female college admissions, while the number of male acceptances has flatlined.
- Have higher college graduation rates.

Compared with girls, on the other hand, boys are more likely to:

- Die in an accident before they reach the age of twenty.
- Be diagnosed with mental, emotional, learning, or behavioral problems.

- Repeat a grade in elementary school.
- Be suspended, expelled, or drop out of school.

These statistics are sobering, but is there really a crisis? Whitmire and others may be viewing the situation from the wrong perspective. Instead of a downward trend for males, we are in the midst of something positive for girls. There is nothing new about the academic gender gap—girls have done better than boys since education became compulsory about a hundred years ago! What has changed is that more females are going to college, with their eye on a PhD. Greater opportunity for women means more competition for men.

The fact remains, however, that boys fare worse in school. Why? And what does this mean for your opt-out? To answer these questions, let's take another look at the brain, with a focus on the different ways that boys and girls learn.

His and Hers Brains

Gender difference is a hot topic! It has been highly politicized since the early 1970s, when feminism gained momentum. Since then significant strides have been made to advance women toward jobs with higher pay and status. Today, however, there is a backlash. For example, the subtitle of Hoff Sommers's book *The War Against Boys* is *How Misguided Feminism Is Harming Young Men*. In her book, she writes that schools are "an inhospitable environment for boys, because they are forced to conform to a regime of obedience." More succinctly put, Hoff Sommers believes that schools emasculate boys. Others argue that boys' and girls' brains are so dissimilar that they should be parented and educated in different ways.

This subject has generated a lot of controversy. The discovery of even the smallest research finding is quickly picked up in the media and exaggerated substantially out of proportion: "Girls Have More Empathy than Boys!" "Women Are Better Multitaskers than Men" and the like are typical headlines. Worse, arguments justifying a boy crisis or advocating for same-sex education are sometimes based on poorly designed research, or take research findings so far out of context that even the primary investigator yells "foul." Unfortunately all this hyperbole reinforces gender stereotypes that harm girls *and* boys.

The truth is that boys' and girls' brains are more similar than they are different—according to Dr. Lise Eliot, that is. In her well-researched book *Pink Brain, Blue Brain: How Small Differences Grow into Troublesome Gaps—And What We Can Do About It*, Dr. Eliot, an associate professor of neuroscience at the Rosalind Franklin University of Medicine and Science, writes: "What I've found, after an exhaustive search, was surprisingly little solid evidence of sex differences in children's brains." Boys and girls might develop verbal, nonverbal, motor, and emotional abilities at a different pace, or in a different order, but ultimately they end up in the same place.

However, Dr. Eliot does describe small gender differences that begin as "little seeds planted by genes and hormones." These seeds are then amplified over time by practice, parental expectations, and a child's own strong need to conform to gender stereotypes. Parents play a huge role in shaping boys to be boys and girls to be girls. For example, in one study parents of newborn girls described their new addition as more delicate, weaker, and prettier than did parents of newborn bouncing baby boys. In another study baby girls who were dressed as boys were described by adults, who were not in on the ruse, as angrier than when the adult knew the baby's real gender. And even mothers who pay attention to their children's feelings tend to ignore boys' expression of pain (remember, big boys don't cry) and girls' expression of anger.

Though boys and girls are equally ready to start kindergarten, the demands of a traditional classroom (to sit still and listen) do play to a girl's strengths. Let's take a closer look to see how, for some boys, these subtle differences can turn some boys off school from the beginning.

Motor Skills

Motor skills come in two flavors—big and small. Big motor (aka gross) skills include crawling, walking, running, skipping, hopping, and so on. Boys and girls start life evenly matched here, but because boys are so much more active, they tend to get more practice. And practice makes perfect. However, girls have an upper edge in small, or fine, motor skills. Fine motor skills involve not only things the fingers do, like tying shoes or buttoning a button, but also what the mouth does (forming words). While preschoolers are given ample time to run around, as well as to cut and paste, by kindergarten there is less romping and more writing. Here girls have the advantage. Boys with weaker fine motor skills encounter frustration even in kindergarten.

Visual-Spatial Skills

One of the feminist movement's biggest victories has been dispelling the stereotype that boys are better than girls in math and science. While the STEM (science, technology, engineering, math) fields—the concept was introduced by the National Science Foundation in the 1990s—are still male-dominated, girls are steadily catching up. However, boys' visual-spatial skills do develop ahead of girls'. For example, boys are especially good at mental rotation, which is the ability to imagine what an object looks like from any angle. This skill comes in handy when building a LEGO® model, or gauging the trajectory of a baseball while standing at home plate. Boys are also better at discriminating between the shapes of different objects and detecting visual patterns. However, the opportunities to apply these skills in early elementary school are limited. Math at this stage requires some visualization (carrying numbers, lining up digits to compute) but is also very linear (reading an equation from left to right).

LANGUAGE

It's widely believed that girls can out-talk boys. While it's true that women may be more chatty then men, Dr. Eliot found that "verbal ability is actually one of the smaller sex differences, equivalent to a mere two IQ points at [age five], and it appears to shrink even further over the elementary years." Nonetheless, by the time they start school, girls do have a slight advantage:

- By nine months of age, girls understand fifty more words than boys, the equivalent of about one month in the development of language.
- Girls gesture slightly more than boys (about 5 percent). (Gesture is thought to be a precursor of speech.)
- Researchers recently discovered that girls perceive sounds more evenly than boys, whose right ear seems more sensitive than their left.

Once again, these small differences might make it easier for the average girl to meet the demands of school than for some boys. Furthermore, these differences could also give girls a slight verbal advantage down the road. For example, girls do not speak more than boys, but they do speak faster. They also rely more on language to create social connections (see chapter 5, page 97). However, by adulthood a man's vocabulary is on par with a woman's, and in sum, the average woman's verbal abilities are only better than 54 percent of the male population. These numbers would not make good odds in Las Vegas.

ATTENTION

Boys may prefer building a volcano model—baking soda lava and all—while girls might do a better job of writing an essay on Mount Vesuvius or Mount St. Helens, but up until now they are pretty much even. However, sitting still is definitely a little girl thing, and it is also a major expectation in the classroom. Perhaps it is unfair to say that boys fidget more than girls; maybe they are just more active. Girls are made of "sugar and spice and everything nice," so of course they have better impulse control than boys. Boys' difficulty with self-control persists into adolescence. In fact, inhibitory control is the largest sex difference between children from three to thirteen years of age. Dr. Eliot concludes that "it is this difference—in the ability to sit still, tune out conflicting impulse's, and focus on completing their work—much more than cognitive sex differences that makes boys' adjustment to school more challenging than girls'."

Girls Versus Boys

A girl's small verbal advantage, combined with her better-developed fine motor skills and inhibitory control, gives her a head start at the beginning of school. While these differences are significant, it is important to keep a few things in mind. First, these findings refer to boys and girls in general, and not *every* child follows these patterns. You may have a girl who loves to play with LEGOs or a boy who loves to read. Second, caution must be taken in applying brain research too directly to human behavior. Neuroscientists don't often agree on how brain structure relates to human activity, and this is especially true when looking at the politically charged area of gender differences. Furthermore, we really can't solve the nature/nurture conundrum. As a result, I have tried to be as conservative as possible—reporting only research findings from peer-reviewed studies, looking for studies that have been replicated, and drawing inferences from behavior that are not too far flung from the findings themselves.

Third, and most important, it is just as likely that a woman will make the next scientific breakthrough as it is that a man will write the next best-selling novel. When it comes to cognitive skills, by adulthood it's individual differences that matter, not gender differences. Even though men and women may take different paths, they both end up at the same place.

School Daze

When I was in early elementary school, I thought girls were smarter than boys because they usually had neater handwriting and turned their work in first. Whenever I lacked a pencil or scissors, which was often, I knew I could count on a girl to lend me a spare. Like most boys, I went through elementary school in a daze. This is because, starting in kindergarten, boys are at a distinct disadvantage to girls.

Think about what it takes to succeed in school—at least in our post-industrial, desks-in-rows version of education. Let's tally the score:

A CLASSROOM SCORECARD

School Expectation	Girls	Boys
Sit still	1	0
Listen to and absorb language	1	0
Control yourself	1	0
Read	1	0
Cooperate	1	0
Total	**5**	**0**

As you can see, it's not looking so good for the boys. And on top of everything else in the chart, girls are much more interested than boys in pleasing their teachers. This difference is rooted in how boys and girls seek status (discussed in chapter 5). Girls do things to enhance relationships, so they are eager to follow directions. Boys, on the other hand, are more inclined to seek a friend's approval by playing the class clown or challenging their teacher's authority. This gender difference is not all nurture—girl chimps are more attentive to their teachers as well. And by that I mean that they're more likely than boy chimps to dig for termites, as demonstrated by an adult chimp.

Boys favor visual presentations of materials (pictures, diagrams, et cetera). Fortunately, educators have moved toward using manipulatives (concrete objects that can actually be moved around) to help teach math, and toward incorporating more project-based learning. Still, there's no getting around the fact that for much of the school day, children are expected to sit and listen. The pressure on boys to become more proficient in the art of sitting still and paying attention begins at an increasingly early age. I was once asked to evaluate a young boy whose writing skills lagged well behind his peers. He was in kindergarten. When I suggested to the school principal that not all five-year-old boys can write sentences and short paragraphs, she replied: "Well, at our school they do." The boy's parents sent him to a different school that was willing to give him reasonable time to develop, and he did just fine.

It's no wonder that young boys often find school both frustrating and overwhelming. I imagine that the farm life experienced by most Americans a hundred years ago better suited boys in many ways, as they could be active all day long. And although ADHD is a real disorder, it might be more relevant to our post-industrial society than it was in an agriculturally based economy. In fact, a recent study took a second, careful look at a group of boys who had previously been diagnosed with dyslexia and discovered that half of them had been misdiagnosed; they didn't have a reading disorder, they simply had trouble sitting still. In *Raising Cain: Protecting the Emotional Life of Boys*, Dan Kindlon and Michael Thompson explain that the "ordinary boy pattern of activity, attitudes, and behaviors are seen by many teachers as something that must be overcome for a boy to succeed in school." The takeaway is that as early as kindergarten your son may have been turned off to school.

The head start that girls get in kindergarten has been found to push them over the finish line by the end of fifth grade. Investigators Thomas DiPrete and Claudia Buchman, who compared boys' and girls' social and behavioral skills, estimate this advantage accounts for 34 percent of girls' higher reading scores and 24 percent of their higher math scores. During elementary school the girls they studied led the boys in "attentiveness, task persistence, eagerness to learn, flexibility, organization, expressing feelings, ideas, and opinions in a positive ways, and showing sensitivity to the feelings of others." However, their real finding was that eighth-grade grades are a better predictor of completing college than standardized test scores! The kids who earned A's in middle school had close to a 70 percent chance of completing college, while a report card with mostly B's brought that likelihood down to 30 percent. The students who got mostly C's had only a one in ten chance of completing college. Now, which gender do you think is getting more A's in eighth grade?

Don't lose hope. This data draws conclusions about a wide sample of students. It does not mean your son is doomed. I know many boys who got B's and even a few C's in middle school (and high school) and did just fine. Boys need time to mature, and their brains need time to develop. Colleges still need to keep the gender balance of their student body as even as possible. Nonetheless, engaging boys in school is a challenge. Let's hear what Chai, Ka'eo, and other experienced teachers have to say about helping boys in school.

Make It Safe

Ka'eo feels that boys need lots of encouragement and validation. Learning needs to happen in an environment of intellectual safety, where they are not afraid to sound dumb or, for that matter, too smart. That's why he lives by the motto "Students need to know how much you care before they care how much you know." Kindlon and Thompson clearly agree: "Boys need to feel full acceptance. When they feel that their developmental skills and behavior are normal and that others perceive them that way, they engage more meaningfully in the learning experience."

As a parent, it's your job to encourage learning and mental curiosity. This means not only tolerating some of your son's strident opinions, but also being supportive if he asks you to, say, edit a paper. It is fine to help him think through *his* ideas (not *yours*), but make sure the final version reflects his voice. If he does let you help, make sure nothing you do causes your son shame.

Likewise, if you get the sense he is being shamed by a teacher, take a stand. I have learned from personal experience that some well-meaning teachers don't realize when they are using shame to shape their students' behavior. A third-grade teacher tried to curb my child's fidgets by turning the desk around. She didn't recognize the embarrassment this caused until we pointed it out and asked her to turn the desk back forward.

Make It Relevant

More than girls, boys have trouble taking schoolwork seriously unless they see its relevance. Daniel H. Pink, author of *Drive: The Surprising Truth About What Motivates Us*, called relevance the fourth R. I could not agree more. Boys ask me all the time, "Why do I have to learn [algebra, history, English . . .] if I will never use it?" Believe me, I've searched far and wide for an answer that satisfies these male teenage skeptics, but I've yet to find anything truly persuasive. Here are a few responses I've tried:

- You may not need algebra, but that is not the point—it teaches logic, error detection, and persistence.
- I don't know why you have to learn it, but I do know that every school in the entire world offers this subject, so someone must feel it is necessary.
- The college you want to get into does not care if you did not like your teacher, or felt you did not need to read Shakespeare. Part of being successful is being able to do things you do not want to do.
- The success of a democracy depends on an educated citizenry. While you might not ever use biology, I want the guy in the voting booth next to me to have enough general knowledge to be able to make an informed decision.

- I felt the same way about math in high school. The joke was on me, however, when I ran a hospital department and had to make a budget.
- The brain is plastic, meaning that it changes as you learn and grow. So when you study algebra, not only are the "algebra" nerve cells aglow, but chemical reactions stimulate nearby pathways that have nothing to do with algebra. So it becomes easier to learn the dates of major Civil War battles or to memorize elements of the periodic tables.
- Your adolescent brain is more plastic now than it will ever be, and it is uniquely wired to learn new things. So cram as much useless information you can in there now, because it's a use-it-or-lose-it proposition. By the time you reach the ripe old age of twenty-five, your brain will seal up the things you have already learned, and it will be harder to get new things to stick.

I hope you enjoy more success with the above responses than I have. In case you strike out as well, I posed the problem to a few teachers, including Chai Reddy. Here is what he had to say: "I wholeheartedly agree with students when they tell me the content they are learning has no relevance. The post-industrial revolution model did work and had relevance, but so much of school today is now outdated—you are this age and will go to this grade, and take this order of classes. Things have changed, but the structures around school have not. So I agree with kids. There are a bunch of reasons it will be relevant, not the content itself, but the process, the logic, the work ethic."

David Murray, a high school math teacher in California, holds a similar opinion:

"I know that I was a punk when I was a student—so I am good at putting myself in their shoes. I try to be real with them. So when they

say they will never use math, I tell them, 'That's true, chances are no one in this room is going to become a mathematician. Ninety-nine percent of you will not need Algebra II beyond this class. However, I would be negligent if I did not teach it to you. That is because 99 percent of you will need to think logically and have a number sense. In the real world you will need to solve problems by rationalizing things quantitatively. Many of you will need to know how to amortize a student loan or mortgage, and 100 percent of you will need to balance a checkbook.'"

David goes on to make an analogy to coaching sports:

"I get that there are things my students don't care about, and that their minds are miles away. But I also coach basketball and football, and I can promise you none of them are going pro. Coaching is about teaching life lessons beyond the court—and the same is true of my math class."

Here's a heartening conversation I had with a fifteen-year-old patient who narrowly escaped failing his freshman year:

ANTHONY: I hate to write. I am never going need to learn how to write. Why do I have to take English?
DR. PRICE: Well that is interesting. What subjects do you think a ninth grader should take?
ANTHONY: Well, math, maybe science.
DR. PRICE: Spanish?
ANTHONY: Definitely not Spanish. When would I ever use that?
DR. PRICE: Let me tell you something. In some countries, at around sixth grade, all the children take a test that determines who goes to college and who does not. The ones who pass the test take classes that prepare them for university. The others

spend their high school years learning a trade, or some other
basic skills. So if you lived, let's say, in England, you might
never have to take some of these subjects. How does that sound?

ANTHONY: I am not sure.

DR. PRICE: Well, let's pretend you have to decide right now
what you want to be when you grow up, and you can only
take the classes relevant to that field.

ANTHONY: I have no idea what I want to be. Maybe go into
business like my dad. So I guess I would take math.

DR. PRICE: Just math? Anything else?

ANTHONY: I suppose a businessman has to know how to write a
proposal or a letter, so I guess I should stick with English class.

At the end of the day it is going to be up to you to talk to your
son about what he is learning and to find the relevance in it. The
only way to do this is to find out as much as you can about what
he is learning. Instead of relying on "How was your day?," ask
him what he learned. Pick one subject, and then let him teach you
a little about it. You might learn something new about the French
Revolution. Ask how he relates to the character in a novel, or how
a history lesson can apply to current events. You can offer your
own thoughts, and you may even want to read (or re-read) some
of the books he is assigned. I loved *The Great Gatsby* and *Lord of
the Flies* more as an adult than when I was in high school.

Ultimately, the goal is to promote intellectual curiosity. To nurture intellectual curiosity in your children, you have to nurture it
in yourself. Bring up things at the dinner table that you wonder
about. Ask your kids what is happening in the world. When my
kids were younger I started every Friday-night dinner by asking
them "What new happened in the world this week?" And read!
Reading is, perhaps, the most important thing you can do to
model the value of learning.

Make Reading Cool

Not every boy is lucky enough to have a teacher like Ka'eo Vasconcellos, Chai Reddy, or David Murray. One thing you can do to make a big difference, however, is to portray reading as a cool activity for boys and men. Bruce Pirie, a high school English teacher in Mississauga, Ontario, points out: "Children in elementary and middle school identify the practice of reading with women. It is the mothers who read books and magazines." Pirie cares so deeply about boys and reading that he wrote a book about it. Bruce knows that for most boys, who have difficulty expressing their feelings, fiction is a turnoff. He hopes, one day soon, to see the reading and writing gender gap shrink, as did the math and science gap—only this time it is the boys who need to catch up. For this to happen, Bruce proposes a simple change in how novels are presented. Specifically, rather than having students first express emotional reactions to fictional works in the classroom, he advocates that teachers start a literature lesson by analyzing a novel's historical context, plot, and themes.

Pirie feels that boys find writing challenging because the process is too ambiguous. Writing requires a heavy dose of "uncertainty tolerance" that makes them feel temporarily inadequate, weak, and not in control. Boys prefer activities that are highly structured and have definite rules. Pirie suggests that rather than "assertiveness training," boys need "tentativeness training." I'll explain how this is done in chapter 12. Until then, if you're a father, and you are not currently engaged in a book, pick one up. Boys rarely see men read anything more than the sports or business page. If your son is in high school, read a book that he might enjoy. Make sure he sees you reading it, tell him a little about it, and then suggest he give it a go. If your son is a bit younger, start a father-son book group. I'll bet you'd be embarrassed to ask friends to join, but that is the whole point, isn't it? You can start by saying, "We are really trying to encourage Jimmy to put down his video game controller and pick up a book . . ." You might be surprised at the positive response you'll get. Read books made into movies and compare the film version with the real thing. Include some nonreading activities like a ball game or camping trip, or plan an outing that's related to one of the books you read. At the end of this chapter there's a list of books your son might find appealing. You can also always check with a librarian— they're experts in what kids like to read.

Help Him Connect to Something Outside of School

If your son is really turned off by school, he may need help finding something unrelated that piques his interest. I have worked with enough opt-outs to form a new category: Mr. Professional. These boys have turned their hobbies into small businesses. One eighth grader took pictures of mountain bikers and snowboarders at local competitions and sold them on the Internet. He became a fixture at the local ski mountain, even earning a free season pass. The fallout from his business venture was a constant tug-of-war with his parents, because he neglected his homework. However, I tend to agree with this kind of entrepreneurial opt-out. In this case I would reassure you that many well-known and successful people paid more attention to nurturing an early passion than they did to schoolwork. David Karp, founder of Tumblr, is a recent example. He started learning HTML at eleven, dropped out of high school at fifteen so he could focus on computer programming, and by age twenty-seven was worth two hundred million dollars. Your son may not be so fortunate in pursuing his ambition, and he still needs to be encouraged to do well in school, but do not underestimate the value of a "hobby."

Get Him Moving

There is no question that boys need to be physical and that exercise helps improve their mood and focus. Richard Louv, author of *Last Child in the Woods*, coined the term *nature deficit disorder* to capture how modern society has turned its back on the great outdoors. British researchers, according to Louv, found that the average eight-year-old could better identify Pokémon® characters than the names of common trees! However, if your son is an "inside kid," I'm hesitant to encourage you to push him out of the house. My aim is to steer you away from power struggles, not into new ones. I have seen few parents succeed in getting their reluctant sons to exercise or work out. If at all possible, though, stop driving him to school. Get him to walk or ride his bike. Lead by example.

Ultimately, strong schools build strong boys. They also build strong girls. Some child experts, such as Dr. Leonard Sax, feel passionately that same-sex education benefits both boys and girls. Chai Reddy, on the other hand, suggests that going to school with girls actually helps boys. I tend to agree with Chai. One study found that, with boys, it's not peers that make a difference, but rather a male teacher. No doubt, we need more male teachers at the middle and high school levels. While the desk-in-rows, one-size-fits-all approach to learning might not be tailored specifically to the needs of boys, it does seem to be the most efficient way to educate the populace, which is exactly the point of compulsory education. However, there are some troubling trends in public education that have more to do with politics than pedagogy, and which are diverting needed resources away from public schools and making it harder for teachers to do their jobs.

My Views on Improving Education for Our Kids

- REDUCE CLASS SIZE. Easier said than done, but this will have the biggest single impact on the quality of education in our schools.
- ELIMINATE MANDATED STANDARDIZED TESTING. Rather than ensure that "no child be left behind," these instruments are killing innovation as teachers are forced to teach to the test. Check out FairTest.org.
- START CLASSES LATER IN THE DAY. Whoever it was that thought a 7:30 a.m. start time and 10 a.m. lunch period was good for adolescents has never met a teenager. Check out StartSchoolLater.net.
- PLAY SPORTS IN THE MORNING. One reason classes begin early in high school is so that students who need to watch younger siblings after school can get home in time. Some districts have solved this problem by holding sports practice before school. This change has an added benefit: Exercise improves attention. It is also a surefire way to build movement into a boy's school day.
- LIGHTEN THE HOMEWORK LOAD. In an effort to raise the international rank of American schools, the homework burden has dramatically increased. However, there is little rhyme or reason to this, other than creating unneeded stress and pressure. Check out racetonowhere.com.

Suggested Reading for Tweens

Series:

Divergent series by Veronica Roth
Maximum Ride series by James Patterson

Ranger's Apprentice series by John Flanagan
Numbers series by Rachel Ward
The Maze Runner series by James Dashner
The Inheritance Cycle by Christopher Paolini
Percy Jackson & the Olympians series by Rick Riordan
The Dresden Files series by Jim Butcher

Comics:

Manga
Naruto *by Masashi Kishimoto*
Shaman King *by Hiroyuki Takei*

Fiction:

Holes *by Louis Sachar*
The Absolutely True Diary of a Part-Time Indian *by Sherman Alexie*
Al Capone Does My Shirts *(and other titles) by Gennifer Choldenko*
A Hero's Guide to Being an Outlaw *(and other titles) by Christopher Healy*
Looking for Alaska *by John Green*
The Chocolate War *by Robert Cormier*
About the B'nai Bagels *by E. L. Konigsburg*

Nonfiction:

How They Choked *(and other titles) by Georgia Bragg*
Guinness World Records *series*

Biographies:
Who Is series (Bill Gates)
Who Was series (Einstein, Galileo)

Sports:

Summerland *by Michael Chabon*

Heart of a Champion *by Carl Deuker*

And don't forget:

Mad *magazine*

Suggested Reading for Teens

Nonfiction:

The Devil in the White City *(and other titles) by Erik Larson*

The Tipping Point *(and other titles) by Malcolm Gladwell*

Bringing Down the House *by Ben Mezrich*

Freakonomics *(and other titles and podcast) by Stephen J. Dubner and Steven D. Levitt*

Tuesdays with Morrie *by Mitch Albom*

Alive *by Piers Paul Read*

Into Thin Air *(and other titles) by Jon Krakauer*

In Cold Blood *by Truman Capote*

Fiction:

Maus *by Art Spiegelman*

The Hitchhiker's Guide to the Galaxy *by Douglas Adams*

On the Road *by Jack Kerouac*

The Boys of Summer *by Roger Kahn*

The Things They Carried *by Tim O'Brien*

The Shining *by Stephen King*

One Flew Over the Cuckoo's Nest *by Ken Kesey*

A Confederacy of Dunces *by John Kennedy Toole*
Fever Pitch *by Nick Hornby*
The Onion Field by Joseph Wambaugh
The Art of Fielding *by Chad Harbach*

Websites:

GuysRead.com
ArtOfManliness.com (100 Must-Read Books: The Essential Man's Library)

From Conflict to Change: The Seeds of Motivation

By now you should be well on your way to achieving a measure of objectivity and empathy for your son's struggles. You understand that your son's lack of motivation is a temporary condition, one intertwined with his emotional and psychological development. You have learned about brain development, and you know that his prefrontal cortex has a way to go before it reaches optimal performance. You also appreciate that school is more challenging for boys than girls, at least through high school, and that the pressure boys feel to defend their masculinity is not relieved by making the honor roll. You recognize that your son's struggle is a normal part of development for many boys, that deep down he has internalized the value of education and achievement and wants to do better. You are now ready to implement a plan to free your son from this eddy and to set him on the path toward self-determination.

The word motivation comes from the Latin word motivus, meaning "to move." According to researchers Deci and Ryan, three basic needs provide the fuel to put the motion in motivation: control, competence, and connection. These are the three C's of internally driven, self-determined motivation. Up until now your son's motivation has come from external sources: his teachers and you. As he matures, however, this role becomes not only untenable but also less desirable. You want your son to set his own goals and possess the motivation to achieve them.

7

The Paradoxical Response and the Plot for False Independence

"Mom, don't you get it?" said the sister of an underachieving
older brother. "Luke's problems are all about control: You try to control
him to do his homework, and he controls you by not doing it."

Despite the best of intentions, you are making things worse for your son. Through a series of false assumptions and reflexive behaviors, you have become the unwitting foil to his success. You have fallen into a blind trap that I call the Paradoxical Response. This trap is hidden by a series of false assumptions about your son, assumptions that by now I have hopefully dispelled, namely:

- Your son is cognitively and emotionally ready to take on all that is thrown his way.
- Your son is not working up to his potential.
- Your son does not care about school.
- Your son is lazy.

Based on these assumptions, you have engaged in superhuman acts to become the engine of his motivation. You've bought in to the misguided idea that with enough oversight, tutoring, and coaching you can commandeer his natural course of development. Now, however, you have made a paradigm shift, and can see the (previously invisible) obstacles that have thwarted your best efforts:

- Your son is still in the throes of emotional and cognitive development.
- The part of your son's brain that is most needed to meet the challenges of high school—the prefrontal cortex—will not be fully wired and insulated until he is twenty-six years old.
- Your son is in the midst of "separating," which means he will rebuke any attempts you make to parent him, even though he still needs lots of guidance and oversight.
- His preoccupation with being "manly" makes him too cool for school and too proud to ask for help.

The Paradoxical Response

Now let me pull you out of this blind trap. The paradox is that the harder you try to motivate your son, the more unmotivated he becomes. At face value, this sounds like he's just being obstinate. However, there is more going on here, and it begins with ambivalence. In chapter 1 you used the ruler exercise to learn that Mr. Bare Minimum is not apathetic about his grades; rather he is ambivalent about trying harder. In chapter 2 you were introduced to the bridge of ambivalence: Crossing it means your son is leaving the dependency of childhood and becoming a self-reliant adult. In chapter 5 your grasp on this conflict tightened when you understood that experiencing dependency not only makes a teenage boy feel like a child but also threatens the masculine identity he's carefully been honing. Your son feigns disinterest to further stonewall you, so you draw the obvious conclusion that he does not care.

However, this is not just his struggle; you have a very large stake in the outcome. Time is running out—there are only a few years left before he will have to fend for himself. Based on the current state of affairs, you fear disaster looms. However, all of your worrying is backfiring. You wish your son was, at least, conscious of his stagnancy: "*I know I have to do my work. But it is so boring and the new Call of Duty just came out. But if I don't bring up my grades I won't get into a good college. But my paper is going to suck . . .*" Maybe he is, but, if so, he's not telling you. Instead, your conversations are curt and unsatisfying:

YOU: Do your work.
YOUR SON: Leave me alone.

What should be an internal struggle between your son's conscience, ambition, and work ethic on one side, and his anxiety, dependence, and self-indulgence on the other, becomes a fight against you.

That is how ambivalence works. Let's do a little experiment to make this clearer.

Ambivalence Takes Turns

First, think of a difficult, life-changing decision you had to make by yourself (which college to attend, whether or not to take a job, whether or not to take a relationship forward). Do you remember going back and forth in your mind, weighing the pros and cons, and feeling that you had absolutely made a decision, only to change your mind an hour later?

Now think of another life-changing decision you had to make

with someone else. Deciding whether or not to have children is a good one. Was there a time when you felt ready to become a parent but your spouse did not? Did you change positions? As soon as your spouse said, "Let's do it," did you get cold feet? As long as your wife or husband held up a stop sign, you were free to imagine what parenthood would be like without really weighing the consequences. However, as soon as this obstacle came down, you had to confront the reality of the decision. This volleying went back and forth until both of you could own the fear *and* excitement that parenthood entails.

Unlike a couple considering having a child, the power struggle between you and your son doesn't switch sides. He's more than willing to unload his anxiety and self-doubt. The more upset you get, the calmer he feels, because you have unwittingly assumed the burden of worrying about his schoolwork and future . . . and he no longer has to. Instead, he can complain about how much you push and prod him. I cannot tell you how many times I have had a young patient say, "My parents are the problem. If they would just leave me alone and stop hiring so many tutors and therapists, I would get my work done." Teens are naturally oppositional; when you step into the trap of the Paradoxical Response, it's like handing your son more ammunition to justify his lackadaisical approach to school. One teen patient put it bluntly: "I did not improve my grades because my father was constantly on my case—in fact all that made me want to do was not do well in school. I learned to work ahead and stop waiting until the last minute on my own, not because he kept telling me to do it."

Something else is happening here, as well. Your son thinks that by rejecting your efforts and rebelling against everything he's been asked to do, he's the one calling the shots. He has given himself an unearned promotion from the apprentice to the master stage of executive functioning. Unfortunately, he's really just engaging you in a vicious power struggle that ensures your continued over-involvement in his life. Primarily he is waging an ingenious plot to postpone adulthood in favor of a prolonged, hidden dependence on you. Because he fools himself into thinking that disavowal of academic success is actually autonomy, I call this "the Plot of False Independence." Done either on the down low or with much fanfare by opting out, he gets you to do all the worrying for him. Though he may outwardly protest your constant surveillance and participation, he's actually forcing you to become even more engaged in his life.

Take Zack, a patient I met several years ago when he was a senior in high school. He had an interesting hobby for a teenage boy, especially in this age of video games and computers: Zack loved to build boats. A curiosity about all things buoyant began when he was a toddler in the bathtub. As Zack grew bigger, so did the size of objects he attempted to make seaworthy. On family vacations at a lake in New Hampshire, Zack would spend hours stringing together pieces of Styrofoam™, wood, and anything else he could fashion into a boat. Eventually Zack befriended a real boatbuilder who began teaching him the trade. By the time Zack came to see me, half of his family's garage was surrendered to his latest project, a sixteen-foot sailboat. There was nothing wrong with Zack's building a boat from a kit, except that in order to do so, he'd given up his schoolwork. Studying never came easily to him because he had both attention deficit hyperactivity disorder and a mild learning disability. He once said to me: "Having a learning disability is like running a race, but everyone is running and you are jumping hurdles." During elementary school, Zack did not resist his parents' help. However, as an adolescent he grew resentful and began to reject their assistance.

In therapy Zack complained bitterly about his parents' overbearing control, and he schemed ways to move to New Hampshire to build boats. But the reality was that Zack's school failure only deepened his dependency on Mom and Dad. Although Zack was very bright, his refusal to do schoolwork ensured rejection from any four-year college in the country. Each night, as his schoolbooks remained exactly where he'd dropped them that afternoon, Zack headed to the garage to work on his boat. His parents stood by, feeling frustrated and helpless as Zack seemed oblivious to the fact that children were supposed to grow up, get an education, and prepare for adulthood. Although they supported Zack's boatbuilding, a college education was non-negotiable to them. Unsure what to do, they cracked down harder, forcing him to go to the library every day after school, checking his work every night, and speaking frequently to his teachers. One day Zack told me, "I don't care about my grades if what I am doing does not make me happy."

Things came to a head one morning when Zack refused to go to school. He did this, I learned in one of our sessions, because he couldn't find his shoes, missed his ride, and "it was all too much to deal with." As Zack told it, the day before he had come home in a fine mood because he had made significant progress at the library on a research project. Later that evening his mother lost her temper about the mess in the house. She began throwing everything Zack had not put away—including his shoes—into garbage bags and moved them into the garage. Zack felt that he could not win; even when he did his homework, he was yelled at for not cleaning up his things. Here's the conversation that Zack and I had:

DR. PRICE: So why didn't you go to school?
ZACK: I just didn't have the energy to find my shoes; I did not want to make the effort.
DR. PRICE: Do you think missing one day of school was enough punishment?
ZACK: What do you mean?

DR. PRICE: Maybe a fair punishment for what your mother did to you would be to miss the whole week from school.

ZACK: Well, I couldn't do that. I'd fall too far behind, but I wasn't punishing my mother.

DR. PRICE: No? How do you think she feels when you miss school?

ZACK: Angry, frustrated. I don't want to give her the satisfaction of my doing well in school.

DR. PRICE: Sounds like a punishment to me.

ZACK: Well, what'd you expect? I go to the library, I prepare for a test, and then I have to put up with this?

DR. PRICE: Sometimes punishment is used to change someone's behavior and sometimes it is used to exact revenge. You managed to make your mother feel as bad as you did.

ZACK: Well, what am I supposed to do? She has all the authority.

DR. PRICE: You found an ingenious way to get back at your parents.

Zack did not yell, "Screw you!" to his parents. He whispered it. They had unwittingly elicited the Paradoxical Response. The more they pushed, the angrier he got, and the less he did. By getting so involved, they made themselves the target of his anger. This fight became a distraction from the real issue that was preventing Zack from getting his schoolwork done. Just calling him unmotivated does not go far enough. Once the adolescent's true feelings of ambivalence are unmasked (and no longer camouflaged behind a power struggle), we can better understand what's going on. Motivation isn't one simple thing that your son lacks. Think of it more in terms of a big, overstuffed suitcase—in order for it to be useful, it must be unpacked.

As long as the Paradoxical Response is in effect, nothing can change. That is why it's useless to work on teen motivation with-out taking your parent-child relationship into account. When you and your teen are embroiled in conflict, you cannot engage in problem solving—especially if the conflict itself is one of the main engines that keeps him comfortably locked in a relationship that allows him to off-load any and all responsibility. Simply stated, the danger of being "the heavy" with an opt-out is that you remain the driving force. Your son never gets the chance to develop his own internal well of motivation, which is ultimately the goal.

Now it's time to change your own behavior. It's time to step out of the way. My plan will only work if you stop worrying about your son's grades more than he does. We'll begin by plotting a new way forward—one that will put the conflict back where it belongs.

Before you turn the page, however, let me tell you what happened to Zack. Zack graduated from high school and wisely took a gap year. He attended a program abroad that allowed him to live semi-independently and attend school. The next year, his freshman year in college back in the United States, did not go well. Zack had trouble keeping up with his course work, failed to complete a few papers, and was placed on academic probation. He chose to take a year off, took classes at a local college, and resumed therapy. That year Zack worked on becoming more independent, which largely included learning to believe in himself as a student. It was not until he was twenty years old that Zack realized that fighting with his parents was actually a way of remaining dependent on them. A year of failure taught Zack that he had to chase his own happiness and not let his parents do it for him. Independence did not come easily—even when he was a college student Zack's parents would question the dean regularly about his grades. Zack did graduate from college, and he's now working toward a graduate degree in special education. Zack's path has contained a few more hurdles than those of his peers, but now, at age twenty-five, he's finally learned how to jump them.

8

Putting the Self Back in Self-Control

Right now you are the lone force behind your son's academic achievement. It is exhausting work—like trying to push a ten-ton boulder that won't budge, no matter how hard you try. The boulder just sits there; it doesn't even break a sweat. And the boulder collects all your dishes in its room, seems to have an endless appetite, and has never been known to roll its way to the laundry hamper, despite having lived in your house for over a decade.

You worry that if he ever graduates from high school and makes it to college, your son will skip all of his classes to play video games, subsisting only on beer and potato chips as his room fills with moldering towels; and that he won't be able to regulate his own behavior—exert the self-control necessary to meet life's responsibilities. And what's more, you know you're partly responsible, but you are caught in a catch-22: The more you do for him, the less he does for himself.

As you learned in chapter 7, your son is winning the power struggle by keeping the conflict exactly where he wants it—outside of himself. But not for long. Though it sounds somewhat medieval, it's time to drive this conflict back inside your son, so that he can face his own ambivalence and find the germ of his own motivation. The aim is to let your son's values, goals, and ambitions fuel his actions. This is the only way that he will eventually find the inner drive to succeed. The qualities you most want him to develop—self-control, self-determination, self-regulation—all begin with the same word. And it is these traits, and not the trophies collecting dust on his shelf, that build self-esteem.

People do things either because they are forced to or because they want to. Researchers Edward Deci and Richard Ryan, who have studied motivation for over thirty years, call the type of motivation behind wanting to do something intrinsic, because it seems to be innate to the person doing the action. Think of the joy and excitement you feel as you're doing one of your favorite things, something that gives you great satisfaction and a feeling of competence. Performing this action does not seem to require any motivation at all.

Obviously there are things your son is intrinsically motivated to do. Could you imagine saying to him, "If you don't turn that video game on you will be grounded this weekend" or "Stop wasting so much time folding your clothes and putting them away"? No, he plays video games and keeps his room a mess all by himself. He finds video games inherently interesting and gratifying, in contrast with his schoolwork. There is little joy in doing yet another math worksheet or memorizing vocabulary words.

But, of course, doing things we do not want to do is an essential life skill, one that requires a great deal of determination. Think of the most determined person you know. (Maybe it's you.) How would you describe them? You are most likely summoning up words like *motivated, committed, focused, hardworking,* and *goal-oriented.* Although the term *self-regulated* probably has not come to mind, as Laurence Steinberg points out:

The ability to control our emotions, thoughts, and behaviors is what enables us to stay focused, especially when things get difficult, unpleasant, or tedious. We rely on self-regulation to stop our minds from wandering, to force ourselves to push a little more even though we're tired, and to keep still when we'd rather be moving around. Self-regulation is what separates the determined—and the successful—from the insecure, the distractible, and the easily discouraged.

The Marshmallow Test

Years ago, the psychologist Walter Mischel showed the importance of a key aspect of self-regulation in his now famous "Marshmallow Test" experiment. At Stanford University's in-house preschool, he sat a group of four-year-olds at a table, put one marshmallow in front of each of the children, and told them that they would get to eat two marshmallows, if they could wait till the experimenter came back. Some of the children were able to wait, while others gobbled up the treat as soon as he left the room. The real significance of this study was revealed years later, when Mischel followed up on the kids. As it turns out, the children who could not wait didn't fare as well as their more disciplined counterparts on a number of measures, one of the most striking being their SAT scores. The toddlers who exhibited self-control scored on average 210 points higher than the gobblers! How could waiting to eat a marshmallow correlate to being successful in life? Actually, it is a powerful predictor. Mischel was studying "delayed gratification," the ability to trade patience and hard work now for the promise of a great reward later.

Becoming Self-Motivated

Rewards and punishments might offer a short-term solution but, in the end, will do more harm than good. Mere compliance is not what you are after. You want your son to *want* to do better—to try harder because it reflects the values you have raised him with, because he cares about and takes pride in his effort. This happens through a process psychologists call internalization, a discovery of Sigmund Freud's. Small children accept their parents' behavior and beliefs at face value. However, as they mature, blind faith will not be enough for these values to retain their hold—your children have to make them their own. According to psychologist Wendy Grolnick, "The process of accepting values and behaviors by actively transforming them into personal values and autonomously self-regulated behavior is called internalization. Once these values and goals are internalized, the child willingly engages in the behavior because of his or her own goals." In other words, internalization is the process of turning external regulation into internal regulation.

This developmental process happens in a series of stages, which are illustrated in the following table.

THE STAGES OF INTERNALIZATION

STAGE	DEFINITION	SOURCE OF MOTIVATION	EXAMPLE
1. Obedient	The child is compliant in order to avoid punishment or get a reward. The child does not independently perform the task—it is only performed if some external contingency is in place.	External	Studying for an exam to avoid getting grounded for failure, or only to earn a good grade. Learning the material is nothing more than a means to an end, and the material is quickly forgotten after the test.

STAGE	DEFINITION	SOURCE OF MOTIVATION	EXAMPLE
2. Conforming	The child now wants to comply with teacher/parent expectations in order to feel worthy or avoid feeling shame or guilt. Motivation is still external. Values have been internalized as "what Mom and Dad want me to do," rather than "what is important to me."	Somewhat external	The student who originally studied to perform well on the exam now studies to feel pride or to avoid feeling guilty for not having studied enough. There is an internal pressure to feel pride and avoid shame. However, this motivation is not strong enough to carry him over obstacles in learning, and he may still give up easily or procrastinate. Likewise, he may also resent the pressure to do things he is not interested in.
3. Identification	The child is now motivated by his desire to be like someone he admires or with whom he feels an affinity. This could be a parent, teacher, or peer. Qualities he likes in these people are becoming part of his identity. He seeks approval of those he admires in order to reinforce these aspects in himself.	Somewhat internal	This student wants to do well on a test because he really likes the teacher, or realizes that his dad was a good student and he wants to follow in his footsteps. This student may still not do as well if he does not like a teacher or finds one class especially boring.

STAGE	DEFINITION	SOURCE OF MOTIVATION	EXAMPLE
4. **Autonomous**	The values and goals have been accepted as the student's own and are integrated into his notion of himself. He takes full responsibility for his actions and performs them because they have meaning for him—whether they bring enjoyment or are the means to a self-determined goal.	Internal	This student is interested in learning, and studies so he can master the material and improve his knowledge and skills. Even if he does not like the subject, he knows that he alone is responsible for earning good grades.

As satisfying as it might be to put the last pile of freshly laun-dered, folded T-shirts neatly in a drawer, you don't do the laundry because you like to. You do it because you care about your family. This action, along with thousands of others, is an expression of a value you hold dear. It is also a behavior that developed over time. Like any other developmental process, progress happens in fits and starts. Take a look at the table with your son in mind. Based on the fact that he does homework only under duress or threat, you would think he is stuck in Stage 1. The truth is, depending on the activity and the day, he may be somewhere between Stage 2 (Conforming) and Stage 3 (Identification). Like every other opt-out I have worked with, he has internalized many of the values you've instilled in him: the importance of education, achievement, and hard work.

The important thing to know is that, no matter where he is in the process, your presence as the external force behind his actions thwarts his progression through these stages. By protect-ing him from struggle or failure, you are preventing him from entering Stage 4. There is only one way to help him discover his

own passions and find the motivation to make them a reality—
that is to take a deep breath, step back, and give him autonomy.
Granted, it will initially feel like throwing a nonswimmer into
the deep end. Still, in the next chapters I will show you how to
create an environment that promotes autonomy but will not let
your son drown.

9

Autonomy—A New Way Forward

In order to grow up, your son needs to form his own opinions and make his own choices—even if he doesn't seem ready yet. To help him, you'll need to begin "parenting forward," treating your son like the man you hope he'll become, rather than continually trying to change the boy that he is. Parenting forward means you will need to stop arguing with his immature self, the one who thinks freedom is the right to be irresponsible. The one who wants to remain a child. It also means you will need to stop trying to rescue him from himself.

It is time for your son to learn that the power to act on his own accord comes with accountability for the choices and actions he makes. Autonomy, the freedom to make meaningful decisions, does not only mean being at liberty to do whatever you want. It also means facing repercussions. In turn, this means being able to manage the anxiety and self-doubt that come with decision making, and to tolerate frustration and disappointment when things do not work out. Bruce Pirie's concepts of uncertainty tolerance and tentative training apply not just to reading literature (see chapter 6, page 129) but also to the entirety of adolescent development. The optimal environment for motivation to grow is one that supports independent thinking and problem solving—in other words, autonomy.

This support becomes vital during adolescence, when the rapid development of abstract thought and self-awareness allows teens to establish their own identities—identities that incorporate the values they have been raised with but also define them as separate from their parents. Any transition to adulthood requires that teens gradually replace childhood dependency with self-reliance.

Dr. Wendy Grolnick, a leading expert on autonomy and parental control, has authored numerous studies comparing the children of overinvolved parents with children whose parents support autonomy. As it won't shock you to hear, she found that the children of excessively involved parents gave up more easily when left to their own devices. They earned worse grades, reported more conflict with their parents, and felt pressured to think, feel, or behave in a certain way. Children from families who value autonomy developed persistence and learned to solve their own problems. They got better grades and felt more positive about their parents than children from overinvolved families. As Grolnick concluded, "When parents support children's autonomy they facilitate children's motivation to master their environments. They also increase children's sense of competence and their control over their worlds, and they increase children's ability to regulate their own behavior."

Other researchers concur. Adolescents who report warm, firm, and democratic treatment from their parents are more likely than their peers to do better in school, because they have a more positive attitude about their achievement. They also report feeling closer to their parents than teens whose parents don't support autonomy. Autonomy in teens has been positively linked to self-esteem, self-confidence, academic achievement, and overall psychological well-being. Less empowered teens lack self-reliance and are at risk for depression and poor self-esteem.

If supporting autonomy sounds easier said than done, you are not alone. In an effort to "fix" their children's academic woes, many, many parents fall into the trap of attempting to take control. Although this approach seems logical, overparenting kills self-motivation by thwarting autonomy.

There is a way to solve this problem, to set expectations and limits without exerting control over your son's internal life—what he thinks and feels. I will address how to provide structure without control in the following chapter, but first let's look at areas in which you might be attempting to wield control without necessarily realizing it.

Emotional Boundaries

Underlying any excessive application of parental control is a lack of respect for a child's emotional boundaries. Boundaries are imaginary lines that define our physical space as well as our thoughts and feelings as separate from someone else's. Boundaries determine what is okay to talk about and what is too private, as well as when it is appropriate to offer an opinion about someone else's choices and when it isn't. If we call people who give unwarranted advice or ask nosy questions intrusive, it's because they are in fact intruding upon or violating another person's emotional space.

Boundaries are a requirement of every healthy relationship, and that's especially true of the relationship between parents and children. A parent who respects boundaries is a parent whose actions communicate respect for their child as a separate and distinct person. "I care about you and love you, *and* I respect that you are your own person, with your own feelings and perspective"— this is the fundamental message of a parent who respects their child's boundaries.

Boundaries set the jurisdiction of responsibility we have for another person's well-being. Parents become intrusive when they get too involved in their children's lives, fail to see their children as separate from themselves, and come to the rescue too often. The closer you are to someone, the more likely it is that you will take on their burdens as your own. There was a time when this type of care was appropriate—when your son was an infant and completely dependent on you. You quickly learned the difference between cries that communicated, "I'm wet," "I'm hungry," and "I'm tired." However, as children mature, emotional boundaries support their growing sense of independence and self-reliance.

The following questions might help you to think about whether the boundaries you set with your teen are appropriate.

- Are you overly concerned or preoccupied with what makes him happy or sad? (Our child's welfare is our responsibility, but there is a difference between care or concern and preoccupation with his every mood change.)
- Do you feel his pain too strongly or get too excited about his accomplishments?
- Do you respect your teen's need for personal and emotional space as he begins to separate from you?
- Do you assume too much responsibility for him?
- Do you respect his privacy?
- Do you maintain decorum even when you are angry? (Politeness is one of the most important boundaries a society has.)

VELCRO® PARENTING

When it comes to overinvolved parents, there has been a lot of name-calling. In addition to "helicopter parents," who hover over their children, and "Black Hawk parents," who swoop down to save the day, there are "switchboard parents," so named because everything in the family must go first through them. In Sweden, overinvolved parents are called "curling parents" because they sweep any obstacles out of their children's paths. Then there are "Humpty Dumpty parents, who are too afraid to allow their eggs to sit on a wall lest they fall off and cannot be put back together again. Recently, Houston Dougharty of Grinnell College warned parents of incoming freshmen against becoming "Velcro parents." Soon I fear we will see a new catchphrase: drone parenting.

This array of nicknames suggests that today's parents really are more enmeshed in their children's lives than parents were in previous generations. My grandfather used to say that he was raised in an atmosphere of "benign neglect." Each Saturday morning he would leave his home in the Bronx, walk down to Manhattan, circle Central Park, and return home by 5 p.m. without being asked by his parents where he was all day. And he was ten! Nowadays, many parents do not even let their ten-year-olds walk to school unsupervised. Mike O'Connor, whom I met when he ran the soccer program in my town, said that back in the late 1950s when he was a boy in Ireland, parents never came to their sons' games; it was not a part of the culture. Now, at least in suburban New Jersey, kids' soccer games are a major social event for parents each weekend, and many become a little too involved. When I coached, I once had to call a parent's cell phone from across the field to tell him to stop yelling directions to the kids.

Parental involvement is by no means a bad thing and perhaps it's not fair to give today's generation of parents such a bad rap. The time and energy we have been able to devote to our children has afforded us a richer relationship with them than we would have had in generations past. Parent involvement is critical to a child's emotional well-being, but you can also have too much of a good thing. While it is possible to be very involved in your son's life and still allow him the autonomy he needs, it's easy to overdo

it. For teenagers who are either unable or unwilling to take ownership of their lives, you must consider how your own parenting may
have contributed to the problem and how it perpetuates the cycle
of overdependence, rebellion, and opting out.

Ms. Fenway is a prime example. Like many parents of unmotivated teenagers, Ms. Fenway felt powerless to elicit her son's cooperation in almost any endeavor. She complained bitterly about
how little work Jasper did around the house and how hard it was
to get him up in the morning and ready for school. They fought
almost every day; Jasper frequently missed the bus and needed a
ride to school. During a family counseling session focused on this
problem, our discussion turned to the subject of clothing—picking
dirty clothes up off the floor and putting them in the hamper so that
Jasper would have clean clothes to wear. By chance, I asked Jasper
how he decided what to wear to school. Without a moment's hes-
itation, Ms. Fenway piped in, "Oh, I lay out Jasper's clothes every
evening." Jasper was fifteen years old! Although Ms. Fenway's situation is extreme, it helps us to understand that underachievement
is not just a "lazy teen" problem; it is a parent-child problem.

Too Much Parenting

Overparenting can take two forms: parents who say too much and
parents who do too much. Of course there are those who say *and*
do too much. Parents who say too much exert unreasonable influence over their children by being too free with their own opinions.
They are constantly jumping in with comments like, "You should
cut the grass on the diagonal—it is so much better than mowing
horizontally" or "You look so good in blue; why don't you wear
your blue sweater instead of the one you have on."

Their favorite words are *should* and *must*, and they feel that
offering criticism is their parental right and obligation. Sometimes they communicate their opinions through body language, a

disapproving glance, or a certain vocal intonation. They often feel that it is absolutely essential for their children to participate in a certain activity, begin a paper in a precise way, or attend a social function. They pursue their agenda with the best of intentions: to promote their child's success and well-being. However, this type of overinvolvement crowds out a teen's ability to form his own opinions and to think for himself.

One teen patient of mine complained when his father tried to hijack a blog his friends and he were creating. "It should be about politics, not sports," said the father, who went on to suggest names and post ideas. That was until my patient set an appropriate boundary—he told his father to butt out.

Parents who do too much jump in too quickly to solve a child's problems, often acting as the child's permanent backstop. They rush every forgotten assignment or uniform to school, call their children in sick to stay home and finish a paper, and diligently do all the chores so their children have more precious time to study. These parents are proud of how much they are willing to sacrifice to help their son.

Throwing kids life jackets is occasionally necessary, but constant rescuing as a parenting style can be debilitating. The child will never learn to solve problems for himself because he is always subtly under his parents' influence. Worse, he gets the implicit message that he *can't* solve them himself. As one teacher recently told me, "Tom's mom and dad help him so much he does not get a chance to learn how to be Tom." The child of a Velcro parent never learns to trust his own instincts, desires, or competence. He also grows up expecting that there will always be someone there to meet his needs, and that things come to him not because he earned them but because he deserves them.

The most successful people are those who can tolerate frustration, anxiety, and confusion. These negative emotions can be powerful motivators. If you have always bailed out your son, made excuses for him, given him third and fourth chances, or done things for him he needed to do for himself, he will never get a chance to experience and overcome those useful frustrations.

Furthermore, when parents—in Madeline Levine's words— "treat kids like royalty, whose only job is to bring honor to the family by earning good grades," they raise prima donnas, not scholars. The word *entitlement* originally referred to a rightful claim to property or possessions. Now it means just the opposite, an illegitmate demand, like your son's assertion that he does not have time to do any chores because he needs to finish his homework.

REWARDS AND PRAISE

Many parents don't realize that rewards and praise can be another way of controlling a teenager's behavior. Although sometimes helpful, the promise of a reward can dampen self-motivation. One of Deci and Ryan's most surprising findings was that offering rewards to people for doing things they found intrinsically pleasing actually decreased their motivation. Others have found that rewards also diminish creativity, along with the ability to think deeply and solve complex problems. Promising your son five dollars for completing his homework can be a short-term motivator—but he will soon get the message that the task is just a means to an end, and that the reward, not the process, is the most important thing. Rewards may improve performance while they are in effect, but they do not lead to a long-term desire to succeed or to achieve.

Nurturing Self-Reliance

Now that the perils of undue parental control are clear, let's look at some corrective measures you can take to support your son's autonomy. Recognize first that autonomy is a gift. Where independence can be taken, autonomy must be granted. Parents ultimately do have power over their children, and this power is slowly transferred to the child over many years (but hopefully not too many) until he is able to care for himself.

It's not easy to stay involved, support your son's autonomy, and set reasonable limits and expectations. However, this may be your most important task. It is certainly the only way to help your son find his own ambition, take more responsibility for his actions (or, when it comes to school, lack thereof), and reengage in learning.

This is the beginning of an important journey. What follows is a framework for supporting autonomy—the nuts and bolts will be fleshed out in the next chapter:

LET HIM CHOOSE. Give your son the opportunity to make his own decisions whenever possible, and solicit his input into the choices you make on his behalf. This is democratic parenting. While he does not have the final say, you do not have to be authoritarian to have authority. Respect his right to have a dissenting opinion.

BECOME A NO-RESCUE PARENT. Don't be so quick to solve his problems for him. Give him a chance. This is especially difficult when he does not take the initiative. However, whenever possible let the world teach him a lesson, rather than you. If he is going to grow up and take responsibility for his actions, he has to face the consequences of his choices and decisions.

LET HIM FORM HIS OWN OPINIONS. And ask him to explain them and tell you why he feels the way he does. You do not have to agree with him, but respect his right to think for himself. There is no need to pressure him to see things the way that you do. Do you still hold all of the ideas you had in your teens and twenties?

Life has probably taught you a few lessons, and it will teach him some as well, if you let it.

LET HIM VOICE HIS OBJECTIONS to a particular activity (like having dinner with his grandmother). It does not mean he will refuse to go. Chances are, if you let him spout off dissent (don't argue back) he will feel better and be more cooperative. It is kind of like complaining to the clerk about how overpriced hot dogs are at the stadium, as you hand him the cash.

BE THE SCAFFOLD, NOT THE BUILDING. Provide him with just enough support to be successful, or even a tad less than successful, so he can recognize his own resources. But remember, metaphorically speaking, it's his building.

When your son is confident that you recognize his right to think for himself, he will feel better about your authority and put up less of a fight. If you are worried that he will grow away from you, keep this in mind: The more he feels that you respect him as an individual, the greater the likelihood he will stay emotionally connected to you.

If you let your concerns about him not growing up and making the "wrong" decisions translate into micromanaging and nagging, you are giving him the message that he cannot function on his own, while simultaneously reinforcing his dependence on you. All of this comes at a cost, including his growing resentment of your involvement in his life. Instead of feeling respected and understood, he feels controlled, coerced, or manipulated. The more space he tries to get, the more intrusive you become. And as you now know, he has a perfect weapon to use against you—a perfect way of expressing his anger and asserting his (false) independence: He opts out.

Let's give your son a better option. When you parent forward, you might be surprised at who shows up in place of your immature, "lazy" son. Eventually he will take all that you have invested and instilled in him and transform it into something completely unique, something completely him.

10

How to Stop Rescuing Your Son and Start Supporting His Autonomy

I t had been a bad autumn for Nick and his parents. Going into junior year, his GPA was just shy of a 3.0, and they hoped (to use a football metaphor) that he could nudge it a few feet farther down the field to win a fresh set of downs. That, they reasoned, would give him many more options when applying to college. Nick got the point, but he had learned long ago to tune them out. What could he say when they asked over and over, "Don't you care about your future?" or "Do you know how much we sacrificed to give you and your brother these opportunities?" "Sure" didn't cut it. His parents' concern about college only intensified Nick's own anxiety. Watching YouTube videos felt a lot better than feeling helpless or guilty.

One Friday morning his parents came down to breakfast and found the following letter on the kitchen table:

Dear Mom & Dad,
You will be receiving a progress report soon. This will not be
going to colleges nor are they my final grades. It is simply to
know where I am at in this point of the year. Please know I have
turned in many of the assignments that are stated as missing. I

*will be taking this weekend to finish completing the rest of the
missing assignments. I would prefer if you kept the concern to
yourselves because I know what I have to do as a student. Thank
you for listening. Anyway I hope you both have a great weekend.
Love you both very deeply. You both did a great job raising me
so far. Keep up the good work.*

Love, Nick

This letter helped Nick's parents to finally take in this message:
To get their son to do more, they had to do less. This is the last
paradigm shift to make, so let's bust a few more myths to help you
ground the overparenting helicopter for good.

Myth Busters

MYTH 1: YOU CAN MAKE ANOTHER PERSON CHANGE
You can't. You might be able to lead this horse to school, but you
can't make him think. Ultimately it is up him. The harder you
push, the more oppositional he will become.

MYTH 2: IF YOU KEEP ASKING THE SAME QUESTION, EVENTU-ALLY YOU WILL GET AN ANSWER
Questions like "Why can't you work harder?" or "Did you do
your homework?" won't get answers, but they will build resentment. You need to learn a different way of communicating with
your son, so read on.

MYTH 3: YOU CAN SHAME OR GUILT SOMEONE INTO CHANGING
There is an old saying: "Don't fix blame, fix the problem." You
already know how damaging shame is to boys—the more you
make your son feel incompetent or inadequate, the more he will

hide behind the mask of invulnerability. To once again quote my favorite parenting writer, Haim Ginott, "When things go wrong it is not time to tell a teen anything about his personality or character. It is time to help." In chapter 4 (page 84) I gave you some mantras to use with your son. Now I have one for you: **Mantra:** *No blame, no shame.*

MYTH 4: YOU ARE RUNNING OUT OF TIME

This is the most paralyzing thought a parent can have: that you have to fix all of your son's problems *today*, or he won't have any chance of making it in the future. This is the fear that leads many moms and dads to become intrusive and controlling. However, none of us can predict how a child will fare, based upon how he acts today, for he still has a lot of growing up to do. Transplant any fifteen-year-old into a twentysomething's life, and failure is guaranteed. My son's first-grade teacher warned us, "It's okay if he cannot sit still this year, but he will be expected to next year." His second-, third-, and, and fourth-grade teachers gave us the same warning. By the time he really had to stay in his seat, he had no problem doing it. If your son is going to learn to regulate himself and fix his flaws, you can't keep taking all the responsibility for them.

An End to Helicopter Parenting—and the Beginning of a Paradigm Shift

It's time to recognize that the old helicopter-curling-drone parent paradigm has to go! Your son is not lazy, but he might be a bit entitled. A good parent is not one who worries all night about what their child needs and then spends all day trying to meet those needs. In our new paradigm, a good parent is one who lets their child struggle with the optimal amount of confusion, frustration, and self-doubt so that he can manage these feelings as an adult. A good parent is one who respects the process of separation and is not afraid to let go. You have been trying to fix the wrong problem, which is why your solutions have not worked. Your son is not lazy or unmotivated. He is ambivalent and entitled. If you help him deal with these underlying emotions, the other problems will take care of themselves. Dealing with ambivalence is a tricky thing; it is very easy to push someone over to side of the conflict you are trying to pull him away from. You cannot be the "defender of change"—you have to be the defender of your son's growing maturity and his ability to make the changes himself. He still needs limits and expectations. However, these need to be communicated with a spirit of optimism. Just like you cheered him on as he wobbled to take his first step, and held back your tears to reassure him the first day of kindergarten would be great, you need to communicate faith in his ability to solve this problem and be successful. The best gift you can give your son is to accept the hormone-ridden, unbridled bundle of energy that he is right now, and trust in his future. Instead of predicting that he will fail out of college, tell him, "I know by the time you get to college you will have figured out how to study." **Mantra:** *Be an advocate, not a prosecutor.*

Remember, there are no quick fixes. This is a process—you cannot rush development, and you have enough time. This process may start today, but it does not end when your son dons his high school cap and gown. In fact, your son's greatest growth may happen in college (and yes, he will get there). **Mantra:** *Make haste slowly.*

MANAGE YOUR ANXIETY. There is no way around the fact that parents worry about their kids. However, separating real concerns from the catastrophes you've imagined will keep you from rushing in too quickly to rescue or control him. Try this: Think about your son's worst-case scenario. Write it down with as much detail as possible. It probably goes something like this: "Never going to college, sleeping in the basement, and spending all day on the couch playing video games." These imaginary disasters distort reality. The antidote is to think them through, using a little logic. Take a look at the chart that follows:

Dealing with the Worst-Case Scenario

Complete the chart below with the worst-case scenario you just wrote down. Like most parents, you might have more than one of these! Then check out the Worry Log in the appendix (page 239) for more help tackling your daily mountain of worries.

WHAT IS THE WORST THING THAT COULD HAPPEN?	HOW LIKELY IS THAT SCENARIO?	SUPPOSE THE WORST-CASE SCENARIO DID HAPPEN. HOW WOULD I COPE?	HOW WOULD MY SON COPE?
He will never get into college and will end up playing video games all day.	Unlikely—there are many different types of schools. He will get in somewhere.	We would get some professional help and insist he get a job and pay rent. Eventually he would get sick of flipping burgers and get his act together.	He would feel terrible that all his friends were moving on in life and he wasn't. This would motivate him to get back on track.
He goes to college, but flunks out.	Unlikely—he will be older and more mature, and might really like what he is studying.	I would remember that many kids go through this, and it's usually a sign that they weren't ready for college. I'd make sure he got into therapy, took classes, and got a job until he could go back.	He would hate it. College is so much more fun than being stuck at home without any friends. His circumstances would motivate him to get back to school.

Strength Inventory

Next, take stock of your son's strengths using the following table developed by Miller and Rollnick. Circle all of the strengths your son displays, even in small quantities, and underline or highlight the top five. These are the strengths he will use to become successful, and the reasons why your worst-case scenario will never come true.

LIST OF STRENGTHS

Accepting	Committed	Flexible	Persevering	Straight shooter
Active	Competent	Focused	Persistent	Strong
Adaptable	Concerned	Forgiving	Positive	Thankful
Adventurous	Confident	Forward looking	Powerful	Thorough
Affectionate	Considerate	Free	Quick	Thoughtful
Affirmative	Courageous	Happy	Reasonable	Tough
Alert	Creative	Healthy	Receptive	Trusting
Alive	Decisive	Hopeful	Relaxed	Trustworthy
Ambitious	Dedicated	Imaginative	Reliable	Truthful
Anchored	Determined	Ingenious	Resourceful	Understanding
Assertive	Die-Hard	Intelligent	Responsible	Unique
Assured	Diligent	Knowledgeable	Sensible	Unstoppable
Attentive	Doer	Loving	Skillful	Versatile
Bold	Eager	Mature	Social	Vigorous
Brave	Earnest	Open	Solid	Visionary
Bright	Effective	Optimistic	Spiritual	Willing
Capable	Energetic	Orderly	Spontaneous	Winning
Careful	Funny	Organized	Stable	Wise
Cheerful	Faithful	Passionate	Stalwart	Witty
Clever	Fearless	Patient	Steady	Zestful

BECOME AN ASKER, NOT A TELLER. Dire predictions about your son's future and directives to study harder go in one ear and out the other. You have been having the wrong kind of conversation with your son, one that only gets his back up. The only way he is going to listen to you is if *you* listen to him first. Teens are especially sensitive to being heard and taken seriously. What you say, or even what he says, is not that important. What matters is how you respond to what he says. If done right, listening can be the best way to express empathy, support autonomy, and encourage independent problem solving. Thich Nhat Hanh (pronounced *Tick Nat Han*), the Buddhist monk and teacher, wrote, "Understanding is love's other name. If you don't understand, you can't love." Your son needs to know that you understand his perspective (even if you don't agree with it) and respect his right to say what is on his mind. It will take time for him to really believe that you are objective, empathic, and nonjudgmental, but this is the only way to get to a place where your son will actually be willing to hear what you have to say. Remember—less is more. The only conversation your son will engage in is one that respects his autonomy. Stay objective and tuned in so you can maintain self-control.

How to Talk to a Teenager

The most important conversation skill you can employ right now **is knowing when to stop**. If your son is fighting you at every step, either your approach is wrong or he is not ready to hear you. Like a Chinese finger trap, pulling (and pushing) harder only causes more resistance. When you see this kind of resistance, it is time to "stop, drop, and roll":

- *Stop* to size up the situation. Is your son escalating the fight, digging his heels in, blaming others, stonewalling you, or just shutting down? If so . . .
- *Drop* your current approach, line of questioning, agenda. Then . . .

- *Roll* with the resistance. Otherwise, he will fight harder. This means stopping the arguing and making a statement that demonstrates that you understand where he is coming from. (More on this below.)

The second most important communication skill is **keeping a discussion going in a productive direction**. To do this, avoid these conversation-ending pitfalls:

- Criticizing and passing judgment.
- Using yourself as an example.
- Minimizing your son's feelings or situation.
- Giving advice.
- Calling your son names like *lazy* and *ungrateful*.
- Giving orders or directives.
- Making threats.
- Persuading with logic, arguing, or lecturing.
- Moralizing or preaching with words like *should*, *must*, or *ought to*.

After reading that long list, you are probably feeling that there is not much left for you to say. Exactly! Follow the rule of 25/75: You talk 25 percent of the time and listen 75 percent of the time.

How to Develop an EAR

To become a good listener, follow the acronym EAR: Encourage elaboration, Affirm, and Reflect. This approach was originally developed by W. R. Miller and S. Rollnick, psychologists who recognized that the key to treating substance abuse is to unlock the abuser's motivation to stop.

ENCOURAGE ELABORATION. Use open- rather than closed-ended questions to get your son talking. Closed-ended questions can be easily answered with a yes or no. An open-ended question requires a more detailed answer.

Closed- Versus Open-Ended Questions

Listed below are closed- and open-ended versions of typical questions a parent asks an opt-out.

Closed-Ended	Open-Ended
Do you want to get better grades?	How do you feel about your current GPA?
Don't you think you would get better grades if you studied more?	What do you think you can do to improve your grades?
Aren't you tired of Mom and Dad nagging you all the time?	Give us some advice on an approach that would work better for you.

Other ways to encourage elaboration include: asking for clarification ("help me to understand," "what else?") and asking for specifics ("tell me three reasons why you hate your history teacher"). You might still get a terse reply, to which you may respond, "Can you say a little more?" But don't probe too much. If your son says more than "fine," "yes," "no," or grunts, you are having a conversation. Here is a sample:

YOU: Tell us where you are with your grades these days.

YOUR SON: Fine.

YOU: Can you say a little more?

YOUR SON: All right, I know I could do better.

YOU: How so?

YOUR SON: It's just hard for me to concentrate on my homework.

Affirm. Set a constructive tone with positive comments that reinforce the fact that you are your son's ally—"*I am glad you said that*" or "*I know this is not easy for you to discuss with us.*" Whenever possible, tie in one of the strengths you identified earlier:

> You: Your dad and I were just saying how much more self-awareness you have developed lately. I see where you are coming from.

Reflect what your son says by making statements (not questions) that reflect your understanding of what he is saying. This is also called mirroring. The simplest reflection restates or paraphrases what your son has said: "*Mmm, it's really hard for you to concentrate*" or "*So you are saying you are easily distracted.*" A deeper reflection takes a stab at what your son might be feeling. For example:

> Your son: Who needs to know what year the Battle of Waterloo was fought?
> You: You really hate history, don't you. You must be worried about the exam tomorrow.

Don't worry about making a mistake. It gives you an opportunity to reiterate your commitment to understand:

> You: You must be worried about the exam tomorrow.
> Your son: Why do you always say that? It's so frustrating.
> You: Oh, I am sorry. I want to get it right. What is it like for you?

Don't be afraid to reflect back your son's negative comments—you are not voicing support for his position; you are just letting him know that you understand.

YOUR SON: I am doing fine in school.

YOU: So you are happy with your current GPA? Help me to understand this more from your perspective.

YOUR SON: There are more important things to me than grades. I am not a nerd.

YOU: So if your grades are not your top priority, what is?

Whenever possible, reflect your son's ambivalence. This will highlight the fact that what he is going through is his struggle, not one you share.

YOU: It sounds like you are not really sure about wanting to do better in school. At the same time, another part of you either does not think you can do better or is not sure you want to put in the effort.

Empathic listening must be done with an open mind and heart. Your son will know if your neutrality and curiosity are not genuine.

You do not have to run through the EAR tenets in any particular order. And you can drop an elaboration, affirmation, or reflection into any conversation, no matter how short. Practice reflective listening with your spouse or a friend before giving it a stab with your son. Who knows, it may improve that relationship as well.

It's Time to Talk to Your Son About School

No doubt you've sat down with your son many times before to discuss his grades. However, I'm guessing that that these conversations have only lead to further frustration and anger. This time will be different. You are almost ready for a whole new approach, one that grants your son autonomy while also holding him accountable. This talk will go much better if you prepare your son for it first (even though he won't know what you're up to). Here's how.

SETTING THE STAGE

Engage your son in one or more informal conversations designed to get him thinking about change. Ask questions here or there, when you think he is most amenable—perhaps in the car, over dinner, or while he is helping you in the yard or around the house (as he should be). Keep things casual—this is a conversation, not a confrontation. Your tone should be curious and reflective. When in doubt, limit your responses to "Interesting" or "I see." Even a vague "mmm" sound will do. Refer back to the ruler exercise from chapter 1 (page 4). Some of the questions you'll be asking, examples of which appear below, are follow-ups designed to jog your son to reflect on his scale of priorities.

"Remember when I asked you to rate on a scale of 1 to 10 how important it was for you to do well in school and how capable you felt of succeeding? You rated your motivation as a 12, but your capability as a 6. What would it take for you to move from, say, a 6 to an 8?"

"What do you think will happen if you make this change, if you get better grades?" This is not a rhetorical question about the merits of studiousness. The answer you receive may in fact surprise you. I've posed this question to patients over the years, and many told me that if their grades improved, they would feel pressure to keep them up. If your son gives you this answer, maintain your neutrality—try an answer like, "Oh, that makes sense."

"What do you think will happen if you don't make this change?" If your son says, "Not much, I will still get into a good college," respond with something like "That's good. I am glad you feel confident" or "I am glad you are not too worried." These are examples of rolling with the resistance. Even if you are not happy with your son's answers, you are still providing him with an important opportunity to reflect on his current situation, and his future.

TOOLS TO SUPPORT AUTONOMY

Here are a couple of good tools you can use to help your son take greater ownership of his academic performance. Use them as part of your preparation strategy.

- THE DECISION GRID. This is an excellent exercise for getting at ambivalence. It involves asking your son to list the pros of working harder in school, and then to list the cons; a fleshed-out version of this exercise appears in the appendix (page 232).
- TAKING OWNERSHIP OF VALUES. Help your son clarify and own his values—the key to intrinsic motivation. Teens like to talk about their values, as doing so helps them assert their own identity. The simplest and broadest question about values is one we often mangle: "Who do you want to be when you grow up?" Replacing the pronoun *what* at the beginning of

that sentence with *who* has yielded some amazing answers from my patients over the years . . . "Someone who takes care of their family." "Someone who is respected by his colleagues." "A kind person."

You might try making values the focus of a dinner conversation, emphasizing how each family member might share some values but not others. Ask family members to imagine they are having a party to celebrate a milestone birthday. Their best friend is making a toast—what would they want it to say about them? What personal qualities do they want to be known for? For more questions along these lines, see Exploring Values in the appendix (page 233).

The Conversation

Now that you have shored up your communication skills, dealt with your own anxiety, and set the stage, it's time to get to the heart of the matter—having a conversation that both sets expectations and supports your son's autonomy. Your job is to provide a framework that sets structure without control. This plan incorporates the idea of scaffolding, which I introduced in chapter 4 (page 77). It is a process of setting expectations, seeing what your son can do on his own, and then fine-tuning the structure until there is just enough in place to produce results.

HERE ARE EIGHT STEPS TO HELP YOU DEVISE A SUCCESSFUL PLAN:

1. STATE THE PROBLEM AND SET THE TONE. As in the sample script below, you'll be explaining to your son that you want to talk with him about school, but you'll be taking a different approach: *"We have been doing some thinking and realize that you are now a teenager, and that it is really up to you to decide what kind of*

*grades you want. We have confidence that you will figure this out,
and that you will be a success in whatever you choose to do. We
know this because every day we see your stengths, the way you
look out for the needs of other people, or apply yourself to your
photography. We also realize that school is important to you, and
know that you want to do better. So here is the deal. We are going
to agree to stay out of your hair. It is your race to run, and you get
to decide what place you want to finish in. However, because we
are your parents, it is still our job to make sure you are running on
the right track, and that you don't come in last. It's also our job to
make sure you stay healthy and get a good night's sleep."*

2. ESTABLISH GROUND RULES.

*"We will limit this conversation to twenty minutes. If we need
more time, we can either agree to continue, or table things until
tomorrow or the day after. We promise not to blame or criticize
you, and or get angry. In return you have to talk. Answers like
'Fine' or 'I don't know' won't work."*

If your son agrees but then doesn't cooperate, end the conversation quickly and schedule some time later or the next day to resume. Stop, Drop, and Roll. You may have to do this several times before he engages. However, keep your expectations reasonable—he is still a boy, after all. Accept terse answers, as long as those answers communicate something.

3. LAY OUT THE PLAN.

Tell your son that you would like to set some academic goals, and that you will give him some time to achieve those goals. If you don't see any progress, you will assume that he needs more time to study, and you will impose some restrictions on his free time. You can't force him to study, but you can help him cut down on distractions.

4. SET GOALS. Ask your son to lay out his goals, in a general sense. Remember, you and he may not have exactly the same goals; the important thing is that he takes ownership of them. Here are some options to choose from—don't attempt to tackle all of them at once.

- Bring up any C to a B and maintain a B average.
- Maintain your current grades, but focus on your worst class—bring that grade up and then work on other grades.
- Complete and turn in homework every day, regardless of the quality. This is one of my favorite goals, because if your son does this, an improvement in grades will follow. When my son was in eighth grade, I asked him why he did not do his homework consistently. He told me, "It's like voting. One vote does not really make a difference—neither does one home-work assignment." My son was, of course, incorrect. Consistently doing homework, at any level of execution, is one of the most important skills a student can have.
- Achieve a certain, specified grade in each subject.

Now you and your son have set out very specific goals. In order for those goals to be effective as motivators they have to be broken down into short- and long-term steps—for example, getting no lower than a B on any test, quiz, or paper. This will be the subject of your next conversation. Give your son the Goal Setter work-sheet from the appendix (page 234). He should spend some time with it, but don't worry if he doesn't complete the whole thing.

5. GET HELP, SET A TIME FRAME. Ask your son if he needs any help to meet his goals—a tutor (if it's within your budget) for a specific class he struggles in, extra help from a teacher, or the like. Then set a time frame. I would suggest working in three-week

intervals, which should be a reasonable amount of time to show progress. Your son might not be able to meet his long-term goals in three weeks, but if he is hitting the short-term targets the rest will follow. Also, agree on the data you will use to measure his progress. Many schools post grades online, though kids consistently complain that teachers do not keep online logs up to date. If that's the case, you can place the onus for obtaining more current data on your son. You can also email teachers, who are usually very responsive. Use both of these tools with caution, however. You do not want to get a daily update on his progress.

6. ZIP IT. It will ultimately be up to your son to figure out what strategies he needs and to get his work done. Don't bring up his grades or monitor his progress unless you haven't seen the agreed-upon data. Don't ask him how things are going or peek into his room to see if he's really working. For many parents, this is the hardest part of the plan. Make sure you and your spouse are on the same page and supporting each other. You might need to line up a "phone a friend" option for those times when you feel the need to intervene.

7. THREE-WEEK ASSESSMENT. Reconvene after three weeks to see how things are going. If your son has shown some improvement, pat him on the back, and agree to meet again in three weeks to see how things are going. If there was no improvement, however, ask him why things did not work out and what he might do differently. Then put some limits in place. Remember, these are not punishments. The rationale for these limits is that because your son needs to devote more time to his studies, you are elimiating a few distractions. Here are some suggestions:

- No screentime during the week, and only two hours on the weekend (screentime includes television, Xbox®, and non-homework-related Internet browsing). To enforce these limits, you might have to have your son do his work where you can keep an eye on him (and his computer). If there is a football game he wants to watch on Sunday, that would max out the limit, so let him know that he needs to plan ahead.
- While he is working, put his cell phone on the kitchen counter, where it will remain until he finishes his work.
- Limit socializing to Friday and Saturday evenings, if he is socially active. Note: I do not recommend this limit if your son has difficulty making friends.
- Impose an earlier curfew so that he will be well rested enough to focus on his work.
- Don't be afraid to set and enforce a bedtime. Teenagers are notoriously sleep deprived. This means lights out, in bed (homework done or not), computer and cell phone charging on the kitchen counter. You might need to buy your son an alarm clock to replace the one on his phone. Yes, they still sell them, and some are deviously desgined to get teens out of bed (like rolling around the room making awful noises until he catches and silences it).

If your son is still in middle school, he might need a shorter timeframe. For younger boys it is appropriate to set weekly goals, get teacher feedback every Friday, and enforce restrictions over the weekend, if goals are not met (for example if you don't turn in every homework assignment you can not watch television, play video games, etc. this weekend).

8. ONGOING ASSESSMENT. After another three weeks or so, check in to assess progress. Even if things are going well, don't revoke

the original limits just yet. Keep them in place for at least three more weeks—or preferably until the end of the semester. If more limits are required, impose them now. Let your son know that if he slips back again, these limits will become permanent. It is also a good time to see if he needs any additional help or if the goals should be revised.

SOME TIPS ABOUT SETTING LIMITS

Setting limits is crucial to enacting your agreed-upon master plan for improvement. It's also incredibly hard for many parents to do—especially when your son pushes back. Punishment might work in the short term, but it involves too high a risk that your son will become more resentful and less cooperative than he is right now. What you need to provide, instead, is structure without control. Think of limits as a fence you build around your child. The fence needs to be flexible, so that it gives him more feedom as he grows. This fence should not be so high that he can't occasionally climb over it—that is how he learns.

Power Struggles: The Black Holes of Parenting

Conflict between you and your son is inevitable. He needs it to separate, form his own identity, and renegotiate his relationship with you. As a matter of fact, arguing, within limits, may actually benefit your teen. Several studies that show teens who experience moderate conflict at home are better adjusted than those who experience either no conflict or extreme animosity.

However, there is one type of conflict you should learn to avoid: a power struggle. Without even knowing you, I can predict who will win the next one: your teen. He will always win. That's because he has so much more at stake than you: He's fighting for his independence. He will best you because he's willing to go to any length to win—screaming, swearing, embarrassing you in public, whatever it takes.

There is only one way to deal with power struggles: avoid them. Do this by offering your son a choice, so that he feels some control. The choice may be to defy you and face a consequence, or to comply—but by offering a choice you are putting the ball in his court and thereby deflating the power struggle. Listed below are some ways teens trap their parents into a battle of wills and how to avoid them.

Common Ways Teens Trap Parents and How to Avoid Them

This table (adapted from Anthony Wolf's book *Get Out of My Life but First Take Cheryl and Me to the Mall*) lists some common ways that your son might engage you in a power struggle. Pay special attention to the column titled Parental Feeling Elicited— that is where the trap is set. These are feelings you might not even know you have that lead you further down into a black hole.

THE TRAP	WHAT THE TEEN SAYS	PARENTAL FEELING ELICITED	PARENT'S FIRST IMPULSE	A BETTER OPTION
Apathy	"I don't care if you ground me."	• Powerless • Helpless	• Increase punishment: "Oh yeah, well then you are grounded for an extra week—see if you like that!"	• Tell your son the limit is still in effect. • Zip it.

THE TRAP	WHAT THE TEEN SAYS	PARENTAL FEELING ELICITED	PARENT'S FIRST IMPULSE	A BETTER OPTION
Defiance	"I am going to the party. You can't stop me." "There is no way I am going to take out the trash." "You can't make me."	• Angry • Disrespected • Ineffective	• Increase punishment. • Reaffirm authority by saying, "You will do what I say, because I am your parent and I'm still in charge!"	• Zip it. • Restate the limit/request. • Offer a choice: "It is your choice: You can go to the party and be grounded next weekend or you can stay home." • "It's your choice: You can walk the dog or leave it for me, but if I do it, I will deduct $5 from your allowance."
Guilt	"It's not fair." "You don't really care about me." "You're a terrible parent."	Guilt—fear that you have done something wrong and that your child will not love you or like you.	• Defend yourself. • Explain how you are "only doing this for your own good. You have no idea how much I do for you." • Drop the limit to earn back the child's love.	Empathize with his feeling: "I am sorry that you feel so poorly treated." Then hold your ground and zip it.

Provo-cation: anger	"You are an asshole." "I can't stand you." "I wish you were dead."	• Anger • Rage • Rejection	• Yell back • Threaten • Add punishment	If the child is complying with the limit, ignore the impulse to say anything, and zip it. If you feel his insult must be addressed, tell him you will deal with that later. "We will deal with the fact that you called me an asshole later, but right now you still cannot go to the party." (Then deal with it later, through either a conversation or another consequence.)
Provoca-tion: sad-ness or self-harm	"You are always criticizing me. You can't stand me." "I am so overwhelmed and anxious right now and you are making it worse." "I am going to kill myself." "I wish I were dead."	• Guilt • Fear • Worry	• Reassurance • Giving in	Empathize with the child's feeling, reassure him that you are happy to talk about this with him, but right now he has to comply with your request (or if he is really upset, have the talk now, but then make sure he complies). This is very manipulative. However, it's always better to be safe than sorry. If your child has a history of depression, or is under the care of a therapist, or if you are truly concerned, call the therapist or make an appointment. Otherwise, you can say, "I know you are very upset, but this is not something we take lightly. If you are really thinking of hurting yourself we need to take you to the hospital." And, of course, if you *are* worried, this may be what you have to do.

GET HIS INPUT. Earlier I said that the best way to support your son's autonomy is to be democratic, warm, and firm. While a family is not a democracy, where everyone's vote counts equally, asking your son to weigh in on family rules will give him a sense of control and increase his cooperation. So will explaining your rationale for making certain rules. Whenever possible, give him the opportunity to make his own decisions. To do this, give some advance thought to where you are willing to give up or share power by using the three-basket technique developed by psychologist Ross W. Greene in his book *The Explosive Child*. Visualize three baskets: In Basket A put all of the issues that are non-negotiable, such as those related to safety (biking without a helmet; going to a friend's without knowing if the parents will be home; staying alone at home while you go away for the weekend). Basket B contains issues that are negotiable, depending on the situation (occasionally extending curfew; wearing jeans when the family goes out for dinner, but not to your niece's wedding). Issues that are really up to him go into Basket C. These can include whether he eats breakfast (or lunch); what he wears to school; whether he goes to a school social. Each family's values dictate which items are Basket B and C issues. For example, some parents feel okay about a pierced ear and others don't.

BE FLEXIBLE, ESPECIALLY WITH HOW STRICTLY YOU ENFORCE CERTAIN LIMITS. If your son consistently makes his curfew but stays out later one night, allowing this to be the exception reinforces your trust in him to exercise his own judgment. However, if you feel he constantly tests boundaries, it is time to tighten things up.

BUT BE FIRM. It's your son's job to push the limits, and it is your job to rein him in. To do so, you must remain calm. It is okay to get angry as long as you don't lose control. Do that, and your son knows that he's gotten the best of you. When you need to impose a limit, explain what rule your son has broken, tell him why his behavior is unacceptable, and state the consequence. Then walk away to establish that you are serious—the matter is closed for discussion.

As Anthoy Wolf has wisely observed, "The best you can hope for is imperfect control . . . a transgression here or there is working 'around' a parent's power, not through it." This sentiment is consistent with the fence metaphor I like to use: Your son is not trying to completely bulldoze the fence—he just wants to climb over it every once in a while. You are still in charge, even if your son is disobedient now and again.

LET THE UNIVERSE DO YOUR HEAVY LIFTING. The best kinds of consequences are those that occur naturally. This is where being accountable for your actions gets real: You don't go to work, you don't get paid. Allow natural consequences to take effect whenever possible. In other words, allow the universe to do your heavy lifting. An unexcused "tardy" followed by a Saturday detention may be far more effective than forcing your son out of bed in the morning. Here are some ways to let natural consequences happen at home:

- Your son refuses to pick his dirty clothes off the floor so you can do the laundry:
  He has to do his own laundry, or wear dirty underwear. It's his choice.
- Your son chooses not to empty the dishwasher when you ask him to do so:
  He still has to empty it, but also do the dishes no one else could do because the dishwasher is full.
- Your son makes you late to work every morning because he cannot get out of the house on time:

You leave on time and let him make his own way to school.
If there is no other way to school, then he will have to take an
unexcused absence for the day. One or two of these and he
will get the message.

Allowing natural consequences to happen at home is acutally a way for you to set boundaries for yourself. These boundaries help you to keep from being taken advantage of. No, you won't do a special load of laundry because he does not feel like putting his clothes in the hamper. No, you will not be late to work each morning so that he can sleep in. It can be especially hard for mothers to set boundaries because of the responsbility they feel to meet the needs of everyone in their families. However, boundaries make for healthy relationships.

SKIN IN THE GAME. Finally, whenever possible, make sure your son has some skin in the game so he earns the things he has. If he wants a new video game, a computer, or even a car, have him get a job or do chores around the house to contribute. An after-school or weekend job teaches kids things they could never learn in school, such as responsibility, how to deal with difficult people, how to be efficient, and how to manage money. A job gives kids a sense of independence—and by the way, it looks just as good on a college resume as being president of the French club.

11

Helicopters, Lawn Mowers, and Drones: Why Parents Control Their Kids

Perhaps you don't see yourself as a "helicopter" or "Velcro" parent—or maybe you do. In either case, self-awareness is a wonderful thing. It gives you the objectivity and empathy needed to help your son. Self-awareness is the only way to keep your own gremlins from affecting your children. Still, the little fiends find a way to creep in. So when you read this chapter, keep an open mind and be kind to yourself.

Love and Fear

Parents become controlling for two very good reasons: love and fear. It goes without saying that you love your children and want the best for them. You don't want them to miss out on any opportunities. You hope they take their talents as far as possible. To that end, you do everything in your power to steer them toward a fulfilling and happy adulthood. The survival of the species depends on it. And, to some extent, so does your self-esteem. We have an evolutionary pull to protect our children, and many parents don't think twice about sacrificing their own psychological and material needs for the welfare of their children. It is adaptive for human beings to be highly invested in parenting.

By the same token, we are hardwired to protect our children from any perceived threats or competition—that's where the fear part of our motivation comes in. Granted, today this competition is for spots on a traveling soccer team or for admission to a preferred college, but a competitive advantage in these areas is what we think it takes to be successful in our society. Because parents love their kids and want them to be the best they can be, many struggle to turn underachievers into slightly better versions of themselves. A colleague of mine coined the term *if-only kids* because she hears their parents continually say, "If only he did a little more homework" or "If only he tried a little harder." Often, however, it's a parent's own challenges and struggles that lead them to become too involved. These are the issues they should be focusing on, and not their son's.

The parent-child relationship is the most complex, intense, and central relationship in our lives. Your attachment to your children is deeper and more complicated than any other relationship because it involves parts of every other relationship you have, including your relationships with your own parents, your siblings, and your spouse. This attachment to your children brings great joy and fulfillment, but it can also cause frustration and pain. Past and future are linked. Many parents hope that through their children (the future) they can free themselves from the past. If this describes you, realize that this hope may cause you to limit who you allow your son to be and what you expect him to accomplish.

A Second Chance

Children are not born perfect. They are not born into perfect families or into perfect lives. Yet we hope for perfection—we hope that they will grow up to be happy, well-adjusted, successful adults.

We hope that they will avoid all the struggles we had to endure. If you grew up poor, you work hard to provide for the material wants of your children and to give them opportunities you never had. If you grew up with the insecurity of a tension-filled house, or had difficult relationships with your own parents, you strive to create a more harmonious environment for your kids. In many ways, having children offers parents a second chance. Not only do you hope that your children will have better lives than you have had, but secretly, or maybe even unconsciously, you hope that they will grow up to become better versions of yourself. Though at face value this attitude may seem selfish, it is also inevitable and unavoidable that you want your children's success—not only for their own sake but also for yours. Without being aware of it, you hope that by raising confident and successful children you will be rescued from your own failings, insecurities, and disappointments. Unfortunately, this wish sometimes causes you to put pressure on your son without even realizing it.

Jake and a Parent's Hidden Expectations

The Bakers are a dramatic example of how a father's best intentions—namely, to protect his son from the suffering he had endured as a child—backfired. Jake was referred to me at the beginning of his senior year of high school. He had been fighting a great deal with his parents, who felt that he lacked motivation and initiative. Jake was the younger of two boys and lived a bit in his older brother's shadow. He earned average grades but was hindered by his lack of confidence. His parents felt that Jake was lazy, and they put significant pressure on him to excel. They were terribly worried that he would not be ready for college.

Although Jake did very poorly in middle school, he improved with each year of high school. By senior year, he was engaged in his studies and working part-time at an ice cream store. Still, he felt that he couldn't meet his parents' expectations. He complained that they were too quick to criticize and too slow to praise him when he did well.

Jake never understood where the pressure was coming from or why his parents did not accept him for who he was. After a particularly difficult fight the summer before he left home for college, Jake asked his father, "Who are you to push me so hard?" He had heard bits and pieces of his father's history—that he had grown up on a farm, gone to community college before transferring to a four-year college, and eventually started his own company. But that was it. In a family therapy session soon after the fight, Jake asked his father for more information about his childhood. What Jake learned that evening was that his father had grown up in a cult-like ashram that his parents joined when he was just a baby. This shed a whole new light on why Mr. Baker was so intense about his son's success. He desperately wanted Jake to have a better childhood than he'd had, and he worked hard to provide Jake with many opportunities and resources. Mr. Baker saved himself through hard work. He was frustrated that Jake didn't push himself more. In speaking about how his own suffering had affected his relationship with Jake, Mr. Baker admitted to his son: "As a parent, you can only escape yourself so much. I did not want to put you through what I went through. I worked so hard to protect myself . . . You got caught up in me needing to prove I was okay through my parenting skills. I do not know if I damaged you."

Parenting and Self-Esteem

Almost everything we do contributes in one way or another to our self-esteem. Whether you are painting a wall, planning a fundraiser, closing a deal, or even writing a book, the better it goes the better you feel about yourself. And the more important the activity is to you, the more it contributes to your self-esteem. Parenting, as I'm sure you're aware, is at the top of the list of important activities. However, there is a difference between feeling good about yourself, as a parent, and relying on these feelings to feel good about yourself as a person. Psychoanalysts have written about the fact that some parents unconsciously look to their children to support their self-esteem rather than the other way around. When this happens, parents lose the ability to see their children objectively or empathize with their needs. Instead of being able to tune in to their children, these parents demand that their children tune in to them.

Keep in mind that such feelings are unconscious and communicated indirectly. A parent never says: "I am sorry I can't really pay attention to you right now because I need you to make me feel better about myself. Do you think you could give me a hug or get an A in school so I can feel I am a great parent and then tell all my friends how wonderful you are? And by that I really mean how wonderful I am." But that is what they may unconsciously wish.

In a much smaller way, these feelings creep into every close relationship. Family and friends *should* make you feel better about yourself—but not exclusively. Things go askew when you depend too much on the admiration, attention, and affection of others to feel worthwhile. This is called narcissism. The parent-child relationship is particularly vulnerable to this type of imbalance, because children are dependent on their parents, and because the relationship is so close.

Think about the thermostat in your home. Once you set the optimal temperature, it makes the furnace kick in when the air is too cold and turns off when it gets too hot. Now imagine a thermostat that does the same thing for your self-esteem. If you experience a slight—say, your friend does not invite you to a party or you don't get a job you hoped for—the self-esteem thermostat ignites, making sure you don't feel these slights too acutely. If this thermostat is broken, however, you need to look outside yourself to feel better again. Now you depend on your family and friends (and other external factors like your appearance) to feel worthwhile and valued. Since you now rely on these outside elements to feel good, you try to control them. Again, this all occurs on an unconscious level, and everyone experiences it, at least a little bit. Controlling parents are really trying to regulate their own self-esteem. They end up controlling their children, by extension.

Saying or Doing Too Much

There is a distinction between the needs of parents who say too much and the needs of parents who do too much. Take a look at the following types of parents who say too much. You'll note some overlap between the categories, and you may recognize a bit of yourself in all of them, or all of yourself in one of them.

THE SIDELINE COACH lives vicariously through their children. They identify too much, not with their child's pain, but with his accomplishments. Sideline coaches are overly invested in their children's achievements. They see their kids' successes as the only way to validate that they are doing well as parents. The sideline coach tends to be competitive, often hoping that their kids will live out their own dreams or accomplish what they could not. These parents not only root too aggressively for the kids from the sidelines, but also put tremendous pressure on them to achieve.

THE PERFECTIONIST. Life is not easy for the perfectionist . . . or for anyone close to them. A high level of achievement comes at the cost of tremendous self-imposed pressure to meet unrealistic expectations. This type of parent is always trying to escape a feeling of inadequacy, hoping that the next accomplishment will prove their worth. Unfortunately, they also expect too much from their family. This relentless need to improve and be the best is draining and causes resentment. It's an inherited problem passed down from parent to child. Perfectionism is caused when a parent's standards for giving approval are too high, or when a parent is emotionally distant. The child keeps trying harder and harder to win their parent's attention and admiration.

THE SELF-ABSORBED parent is too involved in their own life too understand how their son views the world. They are not neglectful or uninvolved, but they can only look at the world from one perspective: their own. They may, for example, be very interested in yoga and try to impart Eastern philosophy to their children, regardless of their children's interests. Like the sideline coach, the self-absorbed parent overly influences which activities their children choose—favoring ones that capture their own interests or that mimic their own childhoods. Often, a self-absorbed parent had parents who themselves lacked empathy, and thus grew up with a deep sense of emptiness. They are like a dog or cat who is continually licking a wound because it doesn't know what else to do.

Parents who say too much indirectly pressure their children to act in ways that will reflect favorably on them. Alice Miller, a Polish-born psychoanalyst who practiced in Switzerland in the 1960s and '70s, wrote a seminal book on the subject. *The Drama of the Gifted Child* was based on her experiences treating talented professionals who, despite their many accomplishments, struggled with feelings of depression and emptiness. Dr. Miller discovered that frequently the parents of her patients were unable to love their offspring "as the person he really is at any given time." These parents were insecure, Miller explained, and lacked an inner ability to feel good about themselves. They had to look to the external world for affirmation, especially to the attention and affection their children gave them. As a result, instead of empathically tuning in to the needs of their children, these parents created a situation in which their children sometimes had to tune in to them, and their children never had a chance to connect to their true feelings or inner passions. They were driven, rather, by their parents' investment in their success. While Miller's patients did not lack motivation, and in fact were quite successful, their accomplishments felt empty because they arose from a need to please someone else.

Now take a look at the three types of parents who do too much.

THE WORRIER feels that their worries will somehow protect their children. They are always on guard for what might go wrong and take constant precautions. They overthink things, are preoccupied with their children's day-to-day lives, and live by the motto that "a parent can only be happy as their least happy child." If they aren't suffering along with their children, they feel as though they are abandoning them. These parents are always running to their children's rescue. The worrier parent works hard to keep irrational fears from holding their children back, but because this anxiety is ever present, their children must become immune to it in order to live without fear.

THE OVERIDENTIFIER takes on their child's problems as if they were their own, and sometimes even gets confused about whose issues are whose. Their kids' struggles may remind them, either consciously or unconsciously, of their own childhood difficulties. They attempt to protect their children from pain that is actually their own and often believe their children have the same troubles they had as children, even though their child's experience may be completely different.

THE SAVIOR feels as though they are on call 24/7. If they don't make themselves constantly available, they feel as though they're abandoning their child. This parent cannot tolerate seeing their child suffer. Rescuing their child is satisfying; it makes them feel always needed and reinforces a constant connection. They tend to wait on their kids, clean up after them, and sweep away as many obstacles as possible. The savior is extremely good at care giving, but becomes too attached to the outcome of their labors. They have trouble caring for their family without being able to control it. Savior parents find it difficult to let go, especially as their children enter adolescence and seek independence. When the child of a savior struggles in school, this need to rescue and control goes into high gear.

Parents who do too much define themselves by taking care of others. They need to be needed. It makes them feel worthy. These are the parents that try to anticipate and fulfill their child's every desire. Again, they don't think, *If I wait on my child hand and foot and make sure he wants for nothing, he will not be able to do anything for himself and will depend on me the rest of his life, until, God forbid, he gets married . . .* However, they habitually do things that their children should be doing for themselves. Feeling needed is one of the perks of being a parent. Parenting is a difficult job, so such perks are really important. When my son's preschool teacher warned us not to carry our children's backpacks for them, I remember thinking, *What's the harm? I like doing this for him.* It's when parents need to be needed too much—when it is the primary way they feel good about themselves—that children grow up feeling powerless and smothered.

Remember Ms. Fenway from chapter 9 (page 160), the mother who laid out her son Jasper's clothes every night? She was definitely a worrier and a rescuer, but for good reason. Jasper had attention deficit hyperactivity disorder and, despite being bright, struggled in school from an early age. Ms. Fenway had to constantly keep Jasper focused on his homework. She became a coach who took over her son's executive functions because he couldn't perform them on his own. Although she got Jasper through elementary school, Jasper became very oppositional during adolescence. It was the only way he felt he could become his own person. But even though Jasper wanted to be independent and make his own decisions, he had significant difficulty separating from his mother, upon whom he heavily relied. Jasper acted out his ambivalence by flinging orders at his mother: "Get me some juice!"; "Mom, make me a sandwich." Although his budding manhood was threatened when his mom took care of him, there was no problem if she waited on him as though he were a king!

Ms. Fenway was overly wrapped up in her son's identity—an example of blurred boundaries discussed in the last chapter. Her own needs overwhelmed her ability to tune in to her son's independent strivings, resulting in Jasper's lack of responsibility and ownership of his life.

A Self-Perpetuating Cycle

Although there is no gene for it, narcissism is inherited. The feelings of emptiness and worthlessness that prevented your parents from tuning in to you as a child may have created the same holes in your self-esteem. Here are some questions to ponder that may help you to sort it out:

1. Have you always been afraid to express your true feelings to your parents, lest you offend them or incite criticism?
2. Has it always been more important to please your parents than to please yourself?

3. Have you ever felt disloyal to your parents when you acted against their wishes or counsel, even if it was what you really wanted to do?
4. Do you feel that your parents don't know who you really are?
5. Do you feel driven? Are you a perfectionist who never feels your best effort is good enough?
6. Are you overly hard on yourself?
7. Is either of your parents overly sensitive to criticism? What about you?

If you answered yes to a number of these questions, perhaps you should examine your own childhood. A good place to start is Miller's book, and a good therapist could also help you further explore these issues.

In Order to Win, You Have to Lose

Parents who depend too much on their children to feel good about themselves have difficulty letting them go. Adolescents are not the only ones who are ambivalent about growing up. The irony of being a parent is that in order to win, you have to lose. If we do our jobs well, our children will grow up and move away. The joys of parenting include a series of bittersweet good-byes. There is the first-day-of-nursery-school good-bye, the first-day-of-kindergarten good-bye, and, before you know it, the off-to-college good-bye, not to mention the thousands of good-byes in between. For some parents, the process of separation is more difficult than it is for others and can stir up feelings of profound sadness and anxiety. Some people struggle to separate from their own mothers and fathers well into adulthood. An adult patient of mine was embroiled in a struggle with her mother about clearing out the belongings at her grandfather's house so that she could move back in. Like Miss Havisham's room in Charles Dickens's *Great Expectations*, the house had been left exactly as it was the day the grandfather died fifteen years earlier. The man's hairbrush was still resting on the bathroom vanity . . . with hair in it! Another patient answered my phone call with the revealing statement: "Hold on, I have to get rid of my mother on the other line." The rest of this woman's therapy was focused on becoming an independent and autonomous adult.

Overinvolved parents often grow up in families where boundaries haven't been well established or are unclear. Members of these families, referred to as enmeshed, are always in one another's business and provide very little privacy or personal space for one another. Enmeshed families have a higher level of conflict than non-enmeshed families. Separation comes at a high cost, because making one's own decisions can be seen as disloyal. Human beings crave unconditional love and acceptance from their caregivers. Those who do not get it have more difficulty growing up and moving on because, as adults, they are still trying to figure out what it is that will unlock that love and make a depressed parent happy or a critical parent pleased, sometimes even long after the parent has died.

The more difficulty parents have had separating from their own parents, the more likely they are to become overinvolved in their children's lives.

Too Much Parenting Creates Too Much Pressure

One of the challenges we encounter as parents is that it's sometimes difficult to separate our own needs from those of our children. The more invested you become in your children's social, academic, and extracurricular accomplishments, the more you try to control the outcome. In turn, children feel an undue and unnecessary level of pressure that interferes with their own intrinsic motivation and enjoyment of a task. There is a difference between making sure that our kids do what they need to do to be successful and staking our own self-esteem on their triumphs.

When you rely too much on being a good parent to feel like a good person, your kids feel it. Your happiness is resting on their shoulders. You may not even be aware of the pressure you are putting on them, but it's there. It may hurt a little too much when they are rejected by a friend, or you feel more disappointment than is warranted when they aren't selected for an Advanced Placement class. Deep down (perhaps buried so far that you are not aware of it) fester thoughts such as *How does this failure or setback reflect on me?* or *It would feel so great to sit with the other parents, knowing my son is on the starting line.*

There is a difference between feeling proud of your son's accomplishments and needing him to excel in order to feel good about yourself. The first set of feelings is about him, and the second set is about you.

Here's an exercise that will help assess how invested you are in your son's success. I thought of it when a patient recounted how crushed her father had been when she chose to attend a college different than his alma mater. She chose Harvard!

1. Pretend that your son was just accepted to Harvard (substitute the top-tier college of your choice). Imagine telling people the news and putting the school's sticker on your car. You might say things like, "I am so happy for him. He worked so hard." Also think about what people must be thinking about you, as a parent and as a person. What would you think about another parent who just told you the same news?

2. Now pretend that your son was just accepted to Adelphi University—a small school on Long Island that has a very

committed faculty. It may be the ideal place for some students (I chose it for this exercise because I went to graduate school there), but it does not have the prestige of Harvard (or the like). Again, also think about what people must be thinking about you, as a parent and as a person. What would you think about another parent who just told you the same news?

3. Now think about the worst-case scenario I asked you to imagine in the last chapter (see page 171). Ask yourself what it would mean for you if your son does not perform well. What would happen if he turned in homework with errors in it? Would it be all right if he missed out on some experience or opportunity? What kind of sideline coach are you, both in sports and academics? Are you like the parent who had to be phoned from the other side of the soccer field because of his sideline antics? Probably not, but many parents worry that failure, any failure, will not only harm their son's self-esteem but also ruin his chances for a bright and successful future. This is an error in judgment. Mistakes are an unavoidable part of life. Confidence does not come from always being successful. It comes from trusting that you can recover from setbacks.

Acceptance

It's not easy to accept your child for who he is at any given moment, if he is not who you want him to be, think he should be, or believe he could be. Given how much you want for your children and how much of yourself you invest in them, accepting a less-than-perfect version of who you want—or even *need*—them to be is very challenging. This is not how you expected things to turn out. You wanted your son to be the best—the best student, the best athlete, the best friend. Acceptance is so hard, in fact, that it can cause us to push, poke, and prod our children in ways that only make situations worse for them. Our fears as parents push us to rob our kids of the very thing they need most: autonomy. Sometimes our issues get in the way. Other times their issues pull us in. In either case, parents can get stuck needing their children to be people they aren't—not completely different, maybe, but just a little different.

It is hard to manage this need for affirmation as you invest in your children and worry about their futures. It is okay to feel good about yourself when your children do well, but your self-esteem should not depend on their accomplishments. It is okay to enjoy their achievements, but it is not okay to live through them. It is okay to worry about your children and push them, but it is not okay to control them. How do you know, then, how much is too much, especially if your teen has decided to opt out? One way is to make sure you keep focused on the goal of respecting your son's autonomy. Another is to be aware of your own needs and make an honest assessment of the extent to which you depend on others to feel good about yourself. You need to think about how much your own parents relied on you to feel good about themselves, and then ask yourself how much of it was about them and not you.

It's possible to provide structure without being controlling, to hold your son accountable without robbing him of autonomy. At this point in his life, he may not be ready to work harder. This doesn't mean, however, that he'll never be ready. In the words of one patient, who struggled throughout high school and college with opting out, "Intellectual ability does not equal intellectual capability." And in the words of the poet Kahlil Gibran, from *The Prophet*:

Your children are not your children.
They are the sons and daughters of Life's longing for itself.
They come through you but not from you,
And though they are with you yet they belong not to you.

You may give them your love but not your thoughts,
For they have their own thoughts.
You may house their bodies but not their souls,
For their souls dwell in the house of tomorrow,
        which you cannot visit, not even in your dreams.
You may strive to be like them, but seek not to make them like you.
For life goes not backward nor tarries with yesterday.

—"On Children," Gibran, 1923

12

I Think I Can

If your son could really "do school," he would jump out of bed each morning eager to start the day. Maybe you see him do this on the weekend, or from June through August, but never on a school day. If doing school were only about intelligence, your son might like it better. But it's not. It takes tremendous willpower to stay focused through classes that seem irrelevant, only to come home and wade through hours of boring homework. It also takes skill to keep organized, memorize facts and formulas, and write papers. If your son felt more competent in these areas, he might be more motivated.

Gaining competence takes elbow grease and a willingness to fail: to fall down the ski hill, burn a cake, write a terrible poem, or strike out. In order to learn, you have to bear feeling ignorant, unskilled, and even foolish. People who feel competent have a lot of uncertainty tolerance. The problem is that by opting out, your son is robbing himself of invaluable opportunities. He needs to feel more competent at being incompetent.

It's probably been a while since you have experienced the stumbles and slipups that come with learning. As adults, opportunities to try something new are rare. So before going any further, complete this exercise to remind yourself what incompetence feels like:

- Think of something that you are good at. It might be a sport, an academic subject, or a talent such as playing an instrument, cooking, or the like. Now recall what it was like when you were first learning to do this thing. What kept you going? Did it come completely naturally to you? Were there frustrating moments along the way? How did you overcome them?
- Now recall something that you have never been good at. Did you give up without really trying or did you keep at it until you got a little better? Imagine yourself doing this thing while others are watching. How does it feel?
- Finally, think about any recent experience that took you out of your comfort zone. Perhaps you took up tennis, got a work assignment that required new skills, or volunteered to chair a fund-raiser you've never done before. How did you feel going in? What were the obstacles you faced? How did you learn to master this new endeavor?

Building Competence

Now that you have finely tuned your empathy for your son, let's get him on the right track—one that increases uncertainty tolerance and builds competence. Chances are that you've already read one of the best books written on the subject—probably more than once. It's *The Little Engine That Could*, the story of a poor little train engine who initially didn't think she had what it would take to haul cars loaded with goodies over the mountain. However, somewhere along the way, that little engine was transformed from the little engine that couldn't into the little engine that could. The author doesn't explain exactly what changes the engine's mind, but nowhere in the story is there a mommy or daddy train saying, "If you don't get over that mountain you will be grounded for the weekend."

The little engine's secret fuel is known in the field of psychology as self-efficacy. Psychologists have been studying it—and its relationship to success—for decades. In lay terms, self-efficacy is defined as a person's belief in their ability to succeed. People who *believe* they can do better, *do* better. It's really that simple. Self-efficacy is like a turbocharge that kicks in when the going gets rough. People with self-efficacy are better able to face obstacles and tolerate disappointment because they attribute failure to something in their control. They feel competent being incompetent knowing that effort, practice, and new skills will bring success. Students who lack self-efficacy become overwhelmed and filled with self-doubt when they are stumped or challenged. In a way, students with self-efficacy are not better at working; they are better at failing.

Carol Dweck, one of the top researchers in this area, sees self-efficacy as a mind-set. People with a growth mind-set believe that the harder they work, the smarter they get. Challenge is seen as an opportunity for growth—an opportunity to become smarter, faster, or better—because they can control their effort. Most opt-outs, however, have a fixed mind-set: They are convinced that people are born into this world with only so much intelligence. Effort will not change that, and needing to try is actually a sign of failure. The way they see it, if you are good at something it should come naturally. Dweck and her colleagues found that as students with similar academic success in elementary school weathered the transition to middle school, those with a growth mind-set fared much better than those with a fixed mind-set. The grades of the fixed mind-set kids took a dip at the beginning of sixth grade, and they continued to fall throughout middle school. By comparison, the kids with a growth mind-set were able to steadily improve their GPAs. Dweck concluded that:

> With the threat of failure looming, students with the growth mindset . . . mobilized their resources for learning. They told us that they, too, sometimes felt overwhelmed, but their response was to dig in and do what it takes. Our students with the fixed mindset who were facing the hard transition saw it as a threat. It threatened to unmask their flaws and turn them from winners into losers. And in the fixed mindset, a loser is forever. It's no wonder that many adolescents mobilize their resources, not for learning, but to protect their egos. And one of the main ways they do this . . . is by not trying.

Mr. Bare Minimum does so little because he interprets frustration as a sign of inadequacy. It's as if he goes through life under a ceiling, visible only to him, that sets an upper limit on his talents, whether they be musical, athletic, or intellectual. He never attempts anything too challenging, lest (in his mind) he hit the ceiling and expose his limitations to the world. What he does not realize is that the ceiling's position is not fixed—it will rise if you bang into it enough. As one of my patients put it: "I would rather lose a fixed match than actually play to win. Because if I then lost, I would have wasted all that effort, and would have exposed to everyone that I am not as smart as they are." Unfortunately, by playing to lose, this young man's fears were coming true: No one ever got to see how bright he really was, so they assumed he wasn't. What's more, instead of wasting effort, he was wasting the opportunity to become even smarter.

Where someone "fixes" their ability has no bearing on the talent itself. The most dramatic example of this comes from another patient, now in his midtwenties, who always felt weak in math. Jeremy is one of the smartest people I've ever met. He went to an Ivy League college and an Ivy League graduate school; in between, he attended Oxford. However, Jeremy is plagued by his perceived math deficiency, so he shied away from anything involving quantitative reasoning for fear his weakness in math would be revealed. Only to me, his therapist, would Jeremy admit the proof that he was a dunce at math—while his verbal SAT score was a perfect 800, on the math section he got a measly 750! As smart as he is, Jeremy needs to gain self-efficacy by changing his mind-set.

To help your son do the same, ask him these questions, which were developed by Dr. Dweck:

1. Do you think intelligence is something very basic about you that can't change very much?
2. Do you feel you can learn new things, but you can't really change how intelligent you are?
3. Is it true that no matter how much intelligence you have, you can always change it quite a bit?

You can also investigate how he feels about any other abilities, such as musical, athletic and artistic ones. Next, explain to him the difference between a fixed and a growth mind-set.

Finally, he will need to be convinced that his brain really can change when he learns new things—in other words, that it is plastic.

THE MIND OF A CABBIE

My friend Mike found out the hard way that younger brains are more malleable than older ones when he wanted to switch careers from his job as an investment banker in London (there is a lesson here about brain plasticity). Never being one to follow the beaten path, Mike wanted to become a taxi driver. Driving a cab in London is very different than it is in Manhattan. Although Mike had already mastered driving on the opposite side of the road, in order to get his taxi driver's license, he would have to memorize every one of the city's twenty-five thousand major and minor roadways. He would also have to know locations of over twenty thousand landmarks, such as museums, hospitals, theaters, and more. As we walked through the city together, Mike pointed out other prospective cabdrivers circling the same blocks over and over, attempting to turn themselves into human Global Positioning Systems and acquire "the Knowledge."

In the end, this enterprise proved more than poor Mike's middle-aged brain could handle. And he's not alone—50 percent of those who take the licensing test fail, and those that pass average twelve tries before they succeed!

Two neuropsychologists at University College London, Eleanor Maguire and Katherine Woolett, determined to use this choice situation (obtaining "the Knowledge" to drive a cab in London) as a research paradigm. They wanted to see if the requirements to pass the licensing test actually created structual changes in the cabbies' brains. In other words, did the cabbies who passed the test actaully become smarter? A group of like-minded subjects went through the same training process as Mike, and were then divided into two groups: one for those who had successfully obtained "the Knowledge" and one for those who hadn't. Before-and-after brain scans would tell if all the learning involved in passing the test created strucutral changes in the sucessful trainees' hippocampi, which, if you'll recall from chapter 3 (see page 57), are the storehouses for memories. Just to be on the safe side, Maguire and Woolett added a control group of average Londoners. As you have probably already guessed (and as they predicted), the trainees who are now driving those famous black cabs thoughout London have more gray matter in a region of their hippocampus than the poor blokes who had to find employment elsewhere. This study proves that people are not born with a fixed amount of intelligence; with enough practice and hard work we really can become smarter.

As for Mike? Maybe he should try becoming an Uber driver.

Turning "the Little Boy Who Couldn't" into "the Teenager Who Could"

Helping your son make the leap from a fixed to a growth mindset is half the battle. The other half is to defeat these enemies of building competence:

1. EMPHASIZING THE OUTCOME. This puts the focus on something your son can't control. Instead, focus on the process. When your son does well, compliment his hard work, and when he doesn't, talk about his disappointment. His achievement should be the product of his effort, not his intelligence. Remember it's not about talent, it's about tenacity, or in the words of comedian Steve Martin: "Persistence is a great substitute for talent." If you focus on the process, your son will never feel like your love is conditional. I recently counseled a mother about her ten-year-old son's confidence problem. She mentioned that she always tells him how smart he is. When I suggested that this might not be the best way to boost his confidence, he piped in: "Yeah, because then I feel like I have to be smart or else you and Dad will be disappointed."

We have already discussed how excessive emphasis on a child's intelligence or talent gives him the message that it is his ability, not his effort, that is the most important thing, and that he has to achieve a certain standard of excellence to win parental approval. Of course, every once in a while, it doesn't hurt to tell your children how smart, handsome, and above average they are (and they are!). But showing too much pride in your son's accomplishments or too much disappointment in his failures can give him the message that your love is contingent on his performance. When children feel that a parent's love is tied to performance in a particular activity, they report feeling compelled to do that activity, and grow to resent this covert form of pressure, as well as the parent who is exerting it.

2. FEAR OF FAILURE. Petrified by today's seemingly high stakes and fierce competition, many parents fear that if their kids fail at anything, they will fall behind. This belief is not only false, but actually dangerous. An old bit between a reporter and a CEO comes to mind:

> "Sir, what is the secret of your success?" asked the reporter
> "Two words."
> "And, sir, what are they?"
> "Good decisions."
> "And how do you make good decisions?"
> "One word."
> "And sir, what is that?"
> "Experience."
> "And how do you get experience?"
> "Two words."
> "And, sir, what are they?"
> "Bad decisions."

Failure is much cooler than it used to be. Every day there seems to be another article praising the founders of a failed start-up for taking risks and initiative. As such articles like to point out, we would all probably still be using typewriters and cassette players if Steve Jobs and Bill Gates hadn't dropped out of college. Not to mention Mark Zuckerberg or David Karp. Your son needs more rope—not enough to hang himself, but a sufficient amount to be able to fall down and get back up. Better he learn that now, while still under your watchful eye, than two or three years from now when he's in college.

3. FEAR OF MISTAKES. Make mistakes a habit in your family. Tell everyone (with as much humor and enthusiasm as you can) about the mistakes you've made . . . and continue to make. Emphasize the lessons learned. Remind your kids why there are erasers on pencils and delete keys on computer keyboards. Here are a few tales of my own mistakes:

- Leaving a laptop in a taxicab (New York, not London). Lesson learned: Don't talk on your cell phone while exiting a cab.
- Losing my wallet (found it in recycling bin on back porch) and checkbook (found it in glove compartment). Lesson learned: Put things away on the merits of where you will find them, not on the merits of expediency.
- Buying concert tickets for my wife's birthday without realizing they were for the TD Garden in Boston and not Madison Square Garden in New York City. Lesson learned: Realizing some mistakes are worth fixing no matter how costly. (I bought the correct tickets on StubHub and gave the others to friends in Boston.)

You can also make mistakes more acceptable by getting out of your comfort zone. Try something new, let your kids see you stink at it, and then make fun of yourself. For instance, you could play against your son in his favorite video game. Maybe your whole family could try something new, so you can all struggle together. My family is nuts about miniature golf. My putts are pathetic, so when my kids were small (and yet badly beating me) I sang them a little ditty I called "I'm a stinky golfer" (sung to the tune of "I'm a Little Teapot").

4. ENTITLEMENT. Competence has to be earned. Overparenting not only gives kids the message "I think you can't" but also provides them with too many opportunities to say, "I think I won't." In asking me to help her son deal with his constant habit of forgetting homework materials at school, one mother related the following exchange:

MOM: You have to use your planner this year. Write down every assignment, and then check it before you get on the bus to make sure you have everything you need. I don't want to have to run you back to school before they lock the doors at three thirty, like we did so often last year. Do you think you could do that?
SON: No.

This mother was as surprised by my response as she was by her son's when I suggested she stop driving him back to school. "And let him go in the next morning without his homework and get a failing mark?" she asked.

"Yep," I replied, "it's the only way he will learn to use his planner."

5. YOUR ANXIETY. Your worrying gets communicated to your son as a lack of faith in his abilities. Think about the message these statements convey:

"You will never get into a good college if you do not bring up
    your grades": I don't think you will get into a good college.
"When you are in college and I am not there to keep
    you focused, you're going to fail right out": I do not
    think you will be able to handle college.
"How do you possibly think you are going to pass chemistry if
    you do not study more for the test?": I do not believe you
    can pass chemistry.

6. HIS ANXIETY. The opt-out is like Dawdle, the eighth dwarf,
and his theme song is "Go slow. Go slow. Away from work we go."
Deep down, your opt-out is afraid; he's afraid of failure, exposure,
pressure, and most of all the future. He deals with this stress by
avoidance. In today's digital world, the distractions are endless:
video games, YouTube, Instagram, Netflix. One teen told me that
his anxiety and his alarm clock get the same treatment: Whenever
he gets buzzed, he hits the snooze button to postpone dealing with
things. However, he wisely added, "As well as this works, it's the
only way I know how to cope." Another patient said, "Whenever I
have a paper to do, I tell myself, 'I'll let future Colin worry about
it. You can trust him.' Then, the night before the paper is due I say,
'That past Colin is such a jerk.'"

Anxiety is like a bully that lives in the back of your head.
Avoidance just gives this bully a chance to go down to the basement and lift more weights. The secret to beating him is to tackle
whatever it is you are avoiding, while being anxious, even for a
little bit. This builds up your "anxiety tolerance muscle" until it
gets strong enough to kick anxiety's butt.

One way your son can really work this figurative muscle is
to keep a thought journal where he can record exactly what
makes him feel anxious while he does his homework. For
example, take a look at the table that follows, which Zack the

boatbuilder (from chapter 7) filled out in my office while he was trying to finish a paper.

The numbers below refer to intensity of feeling, using a scale of 1 through 100: 1 is the lowest level of intensity and 100 is the highest.

ANXIETY LOG

TIME	ACTIVITY	FEELING	1–100	THOUGHT
4:14	Reading	Anxiety	50	I have to write this paper—it's already overdue.
4:16	Reading	Anxiety	50	I started this chapter two weeks ago—I can barely remember what I read.
4:19	Reading	Anxiety	50	I don't think I'll be able to get enough information on the Crusades.
4:22	Reading	Anxiety	75	I can't complete this assignment/I don't want to start the paper.
4:23	Reading	Anxiety	75	Am I ever going to succeed?
4:25	Reading	Anxiety	50	I'm reading too slowly.
4:25	Reading	Anxiety	75	I forgot to walk the dog.
4:30	Outlining	Frustration	75	I want to do something fun.
4:32	Outlining	Anxiety	75	Is the paper going to be long enough?
4:38	Listening to music	Sadness	50	I'm avoiding my work. I can't handle it.
4:58	Listening to music	Anger	75	I've barely made any progress. I just wasted 20 minutes.
5:05	Distracted	Anger	75	I am so mad at Dad for expecting me to finish this today.
5:06	Distracted	Sadness	50	I suck at this.
5:07	Writing	Frustration	75	I hate this $ #@$.

What is amazing about this tool is that even though it took an hour to use it—once Zack put all of his anxious thoughts on paper, his mind was clear to work. You'll find a thought journal in the appendix (page 240).

Being anxious is like looking through glasses that make the world look much more alarming than it really is.

People with anxiety often have a distorted, overly fearful view of the world. Some of the resulting distortions are predictable, and, once identified, they are easy to fight against with logic. As the parent of an anxious son, you can gently point out the inaccuracy in his thinking. This should be done with a reassuring, rather than a correcting, tone.

You already know about the most common type of distortion—catastrophizing (page 170). Here are two others:

- ALL-OR-NOTHING THINKING. Things are never black and white, but this is the irrationality of all-or-nothing thinking. The dinner party you gave was a failure because the broccoli was overcooked; your son had a terrible game because he dropped one fly ball.
- OVERGENERALIZING. This is letting one rotten apple spoil the whole bunch. Just because you did not make the last sale does not mean you are finished. Just because your son struggled through algebra does not mean he will find geometry equally challenging.

The way to challenge these types of distorted thoughts is to make a more realistic and neutral assessment of the situation. It's true that the broccoli was overcooked, but the chicken you served was sensational. Yes, your son missed that ball, but he also got three hits.

And remember: Anxiety may be uncomfortable, but it is never fatal.

13

Connection

Hopefully, you are now more optimistic about your son's academic future than you were when you first picked up this book. You are no longer following the illusory quest for your son to achieve maximum human potential. In fact, the whole idea of imposing this on an adolescent now seems absurd. When you started, however, you were likely troubled by something other than your son's academic underachievement. You felt you were losing him. That wonderful closeness only a parent and child can experience was not just fading into the turmoil of adolescence; it was being fractured by the tension of his poor academic performance. Not only did your son seem to reject your best intentions, dreams, and hopes for him, but he also seemed to disparage some of the values you held dear, the ones that had, until recently, guided your parenting and brought cohesion to your family. How could he not want for himself what you had worked so hard to give him—and which you know every child needs?

While I've reassured you that these worries are unfounded, I cannot offer the same solace about the damage that has been done to your relationship. Connection is the third C of motivation (following control and competence), and the Paradoxical Response is its greatest obstacle. You can't fix the problem without repairing the relationship. The good news is you have already begun. You now appreciate how much your son's thinking has developed, respect the new opinions he is forming, recognize his need to separate, and understand his ambivalence about it. You have ended power struggles, learned to communicate better, and set clear limits and boundaries. You now encourage him to be independent and support his autonomy, all toward the goal of competence building. Most important, you have developed the objectivity and empathy to understand that your son is not lazy at all; he is:

- No longer small enough to have you fix everything, but not yet big enough to solve his own problems.
- Still growing in brain, body, and spirit.
- Following an uneven path of development.
- Unsure of who he is and who he will become.
- Protecting his masculinity.
- Searching for manhood.
- Ambivalent about trying harder and being independent.
- Afraid to fail.
- Worried he is not smart enough.
- Hung up on the idea that others might find this out.
- Unable to tolerate feeling frustrated or anxious.
- Trying to deny that fact that he still depends on you.
- Embroiled in a power struggle with you that gives cover to all of these fears.
- Just as worried as you are about his future, though he may express it differently.

It's now time to make the biggest paradigm shift of all: In order to get your son to opt in, you have to opt out. You have to opt out of saying too much, doing too much, and triggering the paradoxical response. You have to opt out of rescuing him and caring more about your son's academic achievement than he seems to. In other words, you have to redefine your role as a parent, which is not to ensure that your son succeeds, at all costs. Rather, your role is to help him open a path of self-knowledge and growth, so that he can discover it by himself.

Be the Change You Want to See

Here is the kicker: The only way for your son to change is if you go first. The ultimate paradigm shift is to redefine your parental role. Daunting? Yes, but I have already given you a road map. To make this shift you'll need to apply the lessons of this book to yourself. Here's how.

Being a Parent Means Being Competent at Feeling Incompetent

It comes with the territory. Kids do not always respond to your best intentions, and just because you read this book does not mean your son will go along with all of my recommendations. Parenting requires lots of thinking on your feet. More often than not you will second-guess yourself and wonder if you've said or done the right thing. Sometimes it will be obvious—your son will feel calmed by your words or take your advice. More likely, though, it will take days, weeks, or even years before you know the effect of your counsel. One of my favorite quotes about parenting comes from Anthony Wolf:

> You need confidence, and not confidence that you are
> always making the right decision—nobody can do that—
> or that you are always in control of the kid—nobody can
> even come close to doing that. Rather, you need the con-
> fidence that you are the right person for the job and that
> your efforts are definitely not in vain.

If I have learned anything as a parent myself, it is not to trust that my guidance will always be correct, or that my children will make the right choices 100 percent of the time. Instead, what I've learned is to trust the relationship with my kids—that together we can stumble, make mistakes, apologize, and ultimately teach each other things about ourselves that lead to a more meaningful life and a closer connection.

DEVELOP A GROWTH MIND-SET ABOUT YOUR SON

He was not born with a fixed set of strengths and limitations. He will become smarter, faster, and better. You may, however, have to broaden your perspective. Evaluating his progress on a day-to-day basis gives too narrow a view. A different time frame is needed for this: Your son's entire high school experience will be about trial and error, and about testing his limits until he finds they are not set in stone. This is what adolescence is all about.

YOU HAVE TO DELAY GRATIFICATION

Several years ago, writer Jennifer Senior received much attention for her *New York* magazine cover story and book *All Joy and No Fun* wherein she claims that people without children are often happier than their diaper-changing, car-pool-driving peers. For starters, adults without children have a lot more free time and money to devote to their own interests. Parenting is not for the faint of heart. It requires hard work and sacrifice. So, it has to be a little gratifying. There is nothing like the kisses and cuddles of a small child who only wants to spend time with you. Teenagers? Not so much. While you might feel more taken for granted than gratified during these preteen and teen years, it's extremely rewarding to watch your children become more independent and sophisticated.

It's not only normal to feel good about yourself when your child does well, it's one of the rewards for all those sleepless nights.

Taking a self-esteem boost when your child makes the varsity team, gets a lead in the school play, or looks stunning in the new suit you bought him for the family portrait is fine. The problem arises when you depend on *his* accomplishments to feel good about *yourself* as a parent or as a person. This is when you violate his psychological boundaries. Here, delaying gratification means allowing your son to find success on *his* timetable, and not as a condition of your love. In order to do this you have to separate your feelings about your son from your feelings about his academic achievement.

Focus on the Process, Not the Product

Your child's growth is a process. While there are definitive milestones, these should be used as guides, not as goals. If you focus on the process of his development you will never run the risk of making your love conditional. More important, the process is where all the important lessons are learned. For example, while you want your son to comply with the curfew you set, it's more important to consider how you explained your rationale to him, heard his feedback, and, if appropriate, made accommodations. If he breaks it, knowing why, enforcing consequences, and seeing if he complies the next time is all a part of the process. Remember the mantra *Haste makes waste*. The same applies to his grades. They will not improve overnight. It's going to be a process that will help your son develop self-awareness, maturity, and problem-solving skills, all of which will serve him well throughout his life.

Develop Your Own Uncertainty Tolerance

If you want your son to deal with his ambivalence, anxiety, and doubt, you have to tolerate your own anxiety and doubt about *him*, otherwise you will rush in too quickly. This means you may need to let him fail a little bit and give him the space to have his own worries. If you do all the worrying, he will not have to.

A Third Ingredient

In chapter 1 (page 7) I told you about two essential ingredients to help your son: empathy and objectivity. There is one more: compassion—the concern for another's suffering. Connection cannot exist without it. The Dalai Lama said, "If you want others to be happy, practice compassion. If you want to be happy, practice compassion."

You need to develop compassion, both for your son's struggle as well as for your own. For most parents, self-compassion is the hardest skill to master. You must first be patient with your own growth process as a parent—tolerant of the mistakes you've made and with the uncertainty you feel. Remember: No shame, no blame. Your son's opting out is neither your fault nor solely your problem to solve. You can't fix your son, but you can give him the tools to fix himself. Everyone has a different path to maturity. His is still unfolding.

Perhaps the biggest gift you can give yourself (and your son) is to remember that there is still time. The time line to prepare him for adulthood, a time when he will be okay without you, is longer than you think. And even though it seems unfathomable, he is already okay with less support than you are giving him. Remember, your son needn't, and really can't, be completely grown up before he leaves for college.

What Your Son Needs

Here is what your son needs from you, and he needs it now.

COMPASSIONATE LISTENING, where he feels truly heard and understood. Remember to be an asker, not a teller, to follow the acronym EAR (encourage elaboration, affirm, reflect; see page

174). Get him talking by asking open-ended questions and holding back your own opinions and suggestions. Most important, make sure that he feels validated—it is the only way he will trust you and keep on talking.

COMPASSIONATE LIMITS. Your son most definitely needs limits. Here is one last mantra: *Set limits, development happens.* Many parents have no problem making threats, but they struggle to enforce them. Setting clear, consistent, and enforceable limits is one of the most compassionate things you can do for a child. He needs to know you are there, hovering in the background, keeping him safe. He needs to trust that those boundaries will be there, but to also feel that every once in a while he can see what the landscape is like beyond them. He needs to be held accountable for his actions, so he can take ownership over his efforts and decisions.

COMPASSIONATE ACCEPTANCE for who he is right now, not who you think he could or should be. This also means accepting that parenting has its limitations—you can protect, nurture, and guide your son, but at some point he has to take control of his own future. The outcome of good parenting is not an eighteen-year-old who is ready to function on his own—it's an eighteen-year-old who is ready to embark on a lifelong process of growth and self-improvement. In the words of *Washington Post* columnist Michael Gerson, writing about his own experience raising a son:

> Parenthood offers many lessons in patience and sacrifice. But ultimately, it is a lesson in humility. The very best thing about your life is a short stage in someone else's story. And it is enough.

Compassion will help you understand that your son is not lazy. So much of his problem stems from a fear of seeming stupid or untalented. Compassion will help you understand that the problem lies not solely with your son, but rather with a world that asks so much of a boy who will eventually get there but needs more time. Compassion will allow you to trust your son enough to grant him the freedom to learn about himself and find his own motivation and drive. Once he does, even if it takes him longer than it takes some of his friends, this motivation will be truly his, and no one can take it from him.

Too much emphasis on "potential," on a life yet to be fulfilled, keeps us—and our kids—from living and enjoying the lives we actually have. Perhaps, when it comes to our children, the only potential we should be concerned about is the potential to grow and mature.

Then there is this: The joy your son achieves growing toward his potential—that is called happiness. And it will be a wonder for you to behold.

Appendix

HOMEWORK PREDICTOR

TIME PREDICTOR			DIFFICULTY PREDICTOR	
Assignment	How long do you estimate this assignment will take?	How long did it actually take?	Predict how hard this assignment will be on a scale of 1 (easy) to 5 (difficulty).	How hard did you actually find it, using the same scale?

BACKWARD PLANNER

			Due Date:

THE DECISION GRID

DECISION	PROS/BENEFITS	CONS/COST
Improving grades		
Not improving grades		

EXPLORING VALUES

Take a look at the list and circle each item that is important to you now or might be important to you in the future:

Being a good athlete	Being with people	Being loved
Being married	Having a special partner	Having companionship
Loving someone	Taking care of others	Having someone's help
Having a close family	Having good friends	Being liked
Being popular	Getting people's approval	Being appreciated
Being treated fairly	Being admired	Being independent
Being courageous	Having things in control	Having self-control
Having self-acceptance	Having pride or dignity	Being well organized
Being competent	Learning and knowing a lot	Achieving highly
Being productively busy	Having enjoyable work	Having an important position
Making money	Striving for perfection	Making a contribution to the world
Fighting injustice	Living ethically	Being a good parent (or child)
Being a spiritual person	Having financial security	Not getting taken advantage of
Having it easy	Being comfortable	Avoiding boredom
Having fun	Enjoying life	Looking good
Being physically fit	Being healthy	Being a good student
Being a creative person	Having deep feelings	Growing as a person
Living fully	Having a purpose	Having time to "smell the flowers"

Now underline your top five values. What do you think your mother and father's top five values are? How about your siblings'? Now consider which values you actually live by and those you would like to live by.

(Adapted from: smartrecovery.org)

THE GOAL SETTER

STEP 1: WRITE DOWN YOUR GOALS. Start with a long-term goal—the big Kahuna (say, "I want to improve my grades"). Make sure the goal is realistic—if you have a C average, shooting for straight A's is probably aiming too high, for now at least.

_____

_____

_____

STEP 2: WRITE DOWN WHY THIS GOAL IS IMPORTANT TO YOU.

_____

_____

_____

STEP 3: WRITE DOWN HOW YOUR LIFE WILL CHANGE WHEN YOU ACHIEVE THIS GOAL.

_____

_____

_____

_____

STEP 4: NOW BREAK THAT LONG-TERM GOAL DOWN INTO SMALLER, SHORT-TERM GOALS. These need to be specific: "I want to raise my grade in English from a C+ to a B." One long-term goal may generate two or three short-term goals.

1. _____

2. _____

3. _____

4. _____

5. _____

STEP 5: YOU ARE NOT THERE YET—NOW BREAK DOWN THESE SHORT-TERM GOALS INTO SPECIFIC OBJECTIVES. Each short-term goal might have a specific objective, although some specific objectives apply to all the short-term goals. Here are some examples, which you should feel free to use.

- I will turn in all of my homework.
- Every day I will spend 10 minutes per class reviewing and organizing my notes.
- The day I get a long-term assignment I will do something to start it. For example, I could:
    o Write down three possible hypotheses for a paper.
    o Gather a research source.
    o Use a calendar, starting backward from the due date to map out a schedule.

1. _____

2. _____

3. _____

4. _____

5. _____

STEP 6: WHAT IS THE SINGLE THING THAT COULD BE YOUR DOWNFALL IF YOU ARE NOT CAREFUL?

_____

_____

_____

_____

_____

STEP 7: WRITE DOWN WHAT YOU WILL DO IF YOU ARE NOT MAKING ANY PROGRESS.

_____

_____

_____

_____

STEP 8: WRITE DOWN HOW YOU WILL MONITOR YOUR PROGRESS, AND WHO WILL HELP YOU DO IT. Here are some examples:

- I will review this Goal Setter worksheet once a week.
- I will keep track of how well I complete my homework by writing down every assignment (you are doing that already, right?) and putting a check next to every assignment I complete and hand in.
- I will check my grades in every class twice a month.
- I will review this worksheet with my adviser/guidance counselor/favorite teacher and then check in with them every week or so.

_____

_____

_____

_____

STEP 9: WRITE DOWN EXACTLY WHAT YOU WILL GIVE UP IN ORDER TO MEET YOUR GOAL. This is probably the hardest step of all, but something has to change if you have not been successful so far. No pain, no gain. For example: If you want better grades, you might have to find more time to study by cutting back on the time you spend:

- Playing video games.
- Watching TV.
- Hanging out with your friends.
- Surfing the net.

What do you plan to give up? Be specific: State the person, place, and time (for example, "I will give up playing video games every day after school and start my homework sooner"; "I will spend two more hours a week studying"; "I will go to the library and study during my free period rather than going to the cafeteria to hang out with my friends").

_____

_____

_____

_____

STEP 10: SET AN INTENTION. An intention is a course of action you intend to follow. It is an aim that guides your behavior and often gives it a higher purpose. It can also be a positive statement about what you want to experience. Setting intentions can bring greater focus and clarity to your actions and also make them more meaningful. For example, if you set an intention to either learn something new or practice a skill before you start your homework, you will get more from it, and not just go through the motions.

Here are some examples:

- I intend to give more time, more energy, and my best effort to achieve my goal.
- I intend to keep working even when I am frustrated or feel like giving up.

WORRY LOG

DATE & TIME	
WHAT TRIGGERED THIS THOUGHT?	
WORRIED THOUGHT	
STATE THOUGHT AS A PREDICTION	
EVIDENCE TO SUPPORT MY PREDICTION	
EVIDENCE AGAINST MY PREDICTION	
LIKELIHOOD IT WILL COME TRUE	

THOUGHT JOURNAL

TIME	ACTIVITY	FEELING	RATING (1-100)	THOUGHT

Suggested Reading

CHAPTER 3

Steinberg, Laurence. *The Age of Opportunity*. New York: Houghton Mifflin, 2014.

Strauch, Barbara. *The Primal Teen*. New York: Anchor Books, 2003.

Jensen, Frances, and Amy Ellis Nutt. *The Teenage Brain: A Neuroscientist's Survival Guide to Raising Adolescents and Young Adults*. New York: Harper Collins, 2015.

CHAPTER 4

Baumeister, Roy, and John Tierney. *Willpower*. New York: Penguin, 2011.

Fiore, Neil. *The Now Habit*. New York: Penguin, 1989.

Gardner, Howard. *Frames of Mind*. New York: Basic Books, 1983.

Dawson, Peg, and Richard Guare. *Smart but Scattered*. New York: Guilford Press, 2009.

Goldberg, Donna. *The Organized Student*. New York: Simon & Schuster, 2005.

Kolberg, Judith, and Kathleen Nadeau. *ADD-Friendly Ways to Organize Your Life*. East Essex, UK: Brunner-Routledge, 2002.

ADDitude magazine.

ExecutiveFunctionSuccess.com.

ThePomodoroTechnique.com.

Inspiration.com.

CHAPTER 5

Kindlon, Dan, and Michael Thompson. *Raising Cain: Protecting the Emotional Life of Boys*. New York: Ballantine, 2001.

Wiseman, Rosalind. *Masterminds and Wingmen: Helping Our Boys Cope with Schoolyard Power, Locker-Room Tests, Girlfriends, and the New Rules of Boy World*. New York: Crown Publishing, 2013.

Pollack, William. *Real Boys: Rescuing Our Sons from the Myths of Boyhood*. New York: Henry Holt, 1998.

The Mask You Live In (movie). The Representation Project, 2015.

Kimmel, Michael. *Guyland: The Perilous Years Where Boys Become Men*. New York: HarperCollins, 2008.

Marx, Jeffrey. *Season of Life: A Football Star, a Boy, a Journey to Manhood*. New York: Simon & Schuster, 2003.

Brown, Brené. *Daring Greatly: How the Courage to Be Vulnerable Transforms the Way We Live, Love, Parent, and Lead*. New York: Avery, 2012.

———. "Listening to Shame" (TED talk, March 2012), https://www.ted.com/talks/brene_brown_listening_to_shame?language=en.

———. "The Power of Vulnerability" (TED talk, June 2010), https://www.ted.com/talks/brene_brown_on_vulnerability.

CHAPTER 6

Tyre, Peg. *The Trouble with Boys: A Surprising Report Card on Our Sons, Their Problems at School and What Parents and Educators Must Do*. New York: Crown Publishing, 2008.

CHAPTER 12

Dweck, Carol. *Mindset: The New Psychology of Success*. New York: Ballentine, 2006.

Piper, Watty. *The Little Engine That Could*. New York: Platt & Munk, 1930.

Schab, Lisa. *The Anxiety Workbook for Teens*. Oakland, CA: New Harbinger Press, 2008.

McKay, Matthew, and Patrick Fanning. *Thoughts and Feelings: Taking Control of Your Moods and Your Life*. Oakland, CA: New Harbinger Press, 2011.

Notes

CHAPTER 1

If you want to get to know your child better: W. R. Miller and S. Rollnick, *Motivational Interviewing: Preparing People for Change,* 2nd edition (New York: Guilford Press, 2002).

In his book *The 7 Habits of Highly Successful People*: Stephen Covey, *The 7 Habits of Highly Effective People* (New York: Free Press, 1989).

"Who do you see when you look at your child?": Adapted from Tansen Firestone, "Exercise: Who Do You See When You Look at Your Child?" *PsychAlive*, n.d., http//www.psychalive.org/who-do-you-see-when-you-look-at-your-child.

Historian Paula Fass: Paula S. Fass and Michael Grossberg, editors, *Reinventing Childhood After World War II* (Philadelphia: University of Pennsylvania Press, 2012).

CHAPTER 2

Dr. Marsha Levy-Warren explains this in very simple terms: Marsha Levy-Warren, *The Adolescent Journey: Development, Identity Formation, and Psychotherapy* (Lanham, MD, Boulder, New York, Toronto, and Oxford: Rowman & Littlefield, 1996), page 4.

your son's skeleton will increase by 45 percent: Cynthia Lightfoot, Michael Cole, and Sheila R. Cole, *The Development of Children* (New York: Worth Publishers, 2013).

"a boy stops growing out of his trousers": J. M. Tanner, *Fetus into Man: Physical Growth from Conception to Maturity* (Cambridge, MA: Harvard University Press, 1978).

Anthony Wolf, author of: Anthony Wolf, *Get Out of My Life, but First Could You Drive Me and Cheryl to the Mall?* (New York: Farrar, Strauss, & Giroux, 2002).

In the beginning they strive to be "good": Lawrence Kohlberg, *The Psychology of Moral Development* (San Francisco: Harper & Row, 1984).

The sense of right or wrong develops: Michael Thompson, *It's a Boy* (New York: Ballantine Books, 2008), page 255.

According to Michael Thompson: Ibid.

At this stage he'd rather be a "good friend": Ibid.

Lying: Po Bronson and Ashley Merryman, *NutureShock: New Thinking About Children* (New York: Hachette Book Group, 2009).

As Rosalind Wiseman, author of: Rosalind Wiseman, *Masterminds and Wingmen: Helping Our Boys Cope with Schoolyard Power, Locker-Room Tests, Girlfriends, and the New Rules of Boy World* (New York: Harmony Books, 2013).

The personal satisfaction of being honest: Ibid.

However, blindly trusting your son is not wise: Wolf, *Get Out of My Life*.

Michael Bradley, author of the aptly named: Michael J. Bradley, *Yes, Your Teen Is Crazy!* (Gig Harbor, WA: Harbor Press, 2003), page 104.

Your son must divest from seeing you as godlike: Levy-Warren, *The Adolescent Journey*.

He will probably learn more from his bad decisions: Bradley, *Yes, Your Teen Is Crazy!*

Methinks she does protest too much: This is an often misquoted version of the original: "The lady doth protest too much, methinks." William Shakespeare, *Hamlet* (London: Oxford University Press, 1987).

CHAPTER 3

The adolescent brain is uniquely geared to: Laurence Steinberg, *The Age of Opportunity* (New York: Houghton Mifflin, 2014).

A teenager's brain, it turns out: Barbara Strauch (quoting Abigail Baird), *The Primal Teen.* (New York: Anchor Books, 2003).

According to the eminent psychologist Laurence Steinberg: Steinberg, *The Age of Opportunity*; P. R. Huttenlocher, "Synaptic Density in Human Frontal Cortex—Developmental Changes and Effects of Aging," *Brain Research* 163 (1979): 106–54; P. R. Huttenlocher, C. Decourten, L. J. Garey, and H. Vanderloos, "Synaptogenesis in Human Visual Cortex—Evidence for Synapse Elimination During Normal Development," *Neuroscience Letters* 22, no. 3 (1982): 247–52; R. K. Lenroot and J. N. Giedd, "Brain Development in Children and Adolescents: Insights from Anatomical Magnetic Resonance Imaging," *Neuroscience and Biobehavioral Reviews* 30, no. 6 (2006); J. N. Giedd, J. Blumenthal, N. O. Jefferies, et al., "Brain Development During Childhood and Adolescence: A Longitudinal MRI Study," *Nature Neuroscience* 2, no. 10 (1999): 861–63.

However, neuroscientists have another name for it—*plasticity*: David H. Hubel and Thorsten N. Wiesel, "The Period of Susceptibility to the Physiological Effects of Unilateral Eye Closure in Kittens," *Journal of Physiology* 206, no. 2 (February 1970).

the brain is programmed to go through critical periods: Geraldine Dawson and Kurt Fischer, editors, *Human Behavior and the Developing Brain* (New York: Guilford Press, 1994).

adolescence has been termed: Daniel Siegel, *Brainstorm: The Power and Purpose of the Teenage Brain* (New York: Penguin Publishing Group, 2014), Kindle edition, page 93; Steinberg, *The Age of Opportunity*.

In the words of Frances Jensen: Frances E. Jensen and Amy Ellis Nutt, *The Teenage Brain: A Neuroscientist's Survival Guide to Raising Adolescents and Young Adults* (New York: Harper, 2015), Kindle edition, page 83.

The most famous of these dates back: Steve Twomey, "Phineas Gage: Neuroscience's Most Famous Patient," *Smithsonian*, January 2010, accessed May 20, 2015, http://www.smithsonianmag.com/history/phineas-gage-neurosciences-most-famous-patient-11390067/?no-ist.

Dr. Giedd and his colleagues: Giedd et al., "Brain Development During Childhood and Adolescence."

In 1999, when they first reported their result: Sarah-Jayne Blakemore, "Imaging Brain Development: The Adolescent Brain," *Neuroimage* 61 (2012): 397–406.

We now know that the brain develops over many decades: P. Shaw, N. J. Kabani, J. P. Lerch, K. Eckstrand, R. Lenroot, N. Gogtay, D. Greenstein, L. Clasen, A. Evans, J. L. Rapoport, J. N. Giedd, and S. P. Wise, "Neurodevelopmental Trajectories of the Human Cerebral Cortex," *Journal of Neuroscience* 28, no. 14 (2008): 3586–94.

The gray matter of the brain is made up: Jamie Ward, *The Student's Guide to Cognitive Neuroscience*, 2nd edition (Hove, UK, and New York: Psychology Press, 2010), page 18.

Each neuron has up to a hundred thousand dendrites: John J. Ratey, *A User's Guide to the Brain* (New York: Vintage, 2001).

a series of neurons that communicate with one another: Jensen and Nutt, *The Teenage Brain*.

one hundred billion neurons times up to: Ratey, *A User's Guide to the Brain*.

a typical newborn's brain: Ward, *The Student's Guide to Cognitive Neuroscience*.

"the reptilian brain": P. D. MacLean, *A Triune Concept of Brain and Behavior* (Toronto: University of Toronto Press, 1973); Ratey, *A User's Guide to the Brain*, page 10.

However, more complex brain function: Steinberg, *The Age of Opportunity*.

By then, the brain has reached 90 percent: S. Durston, H. E. Hulshoff

Pol, B. J. Casey, J. N. Giedd, J. K. Buitelaar, and H. van Engeland, "Anatomical MRI of the Developing Human Brain: What Have We Learned?" *Journal of American Academy of Child Adolescent Psychiatry* 40 (2001): 1012–20.

Recent brain research revealed that pruning peaks: Steinberg, *The Age of Opportunity*, page 32.

During adolescence, the brain loses 7 to 10 percent: Jensen and Nutt, *The Teenage Brain*.

It coats axons, making the transmission: Shaw et al., "Neurodevelopmental Trajectories of the Human Cerebral Cortex."

This lack of myelination accounts for: Jensen and Nutt, *The Teenage Brain*.

as the gray in a child's brain: E. R. Sowell, P. M. Thompson, C. J. Holmes, R. Batth, T. L. Jernigan, and A. W. Toga, 1999. "Localizing Age-Related Changes in Brain Structure Between Childhood and Adolescence Using Statistical Parametric Mapping," *NeuroImage* 9, no. 6 (June 1999): 587–97; C. K. Tamnes, Y. Ostby, A. M. Fjell, L. T. Westlye, P. Due-Tonnessen, and K. B. Walhovd, "Brain Maturation in Adolescence and Young Adulthood: Regional Age Related Changes in Cortical Thickness and White Matter Volume and Microstructure," *Cerebral Cortex* 20, no. 3 (2010): 534–48; Blakemore, "Imaging Brain Development."

"A slightly unbridled and over-exuberant immature amygdala": Jensen and Nutt, *The Teenage Brain*.

This is why teen boys are so prone: Ibid., page 21.

Abigail Baird, who coined the term *neural gawkiness*: Abigail A. Baird, Staci A. Gruber, Deborah A. Fein, Luis Maas, Ronald J. Steingard, Perry Renshaw, Bruce Cohen, and Deborah A. Yurgelun-Todd, "Functional Magnetic Resonance Imaging of Facial Affect Recognition in Children and Adolescents," *Journal of the American Academy of Child and Adolescent Psychiatry* 38, no 2 (1999): 3195–99.

younger teens actually misperceive emotions: Strauch, *The Primal Teen*.

Referring to the effect of dopamine: Strauch, *The Primal Teen*, pages 134–35.

It's easier to change an adolescent's behavior: Steinberg, *The Age of Opportunity*.

CHAPTER 4

"improve the human genome:" Darwin awards: http:www/dawinawards.com.

***initiate, sustain, shift,* and *inhibit*:** Russell Barkley, *ADHD and the Nature of Self-Control* (New York: Guilford Press, 1997).

"Compared to work with children and adults": Mary Solanto, PhD, personal communication.

The frontal lobes, considered collectively: Jensen and Nutt, *The Teenage Brain.*

As far as the rest of the animal kingdom: Elkhonon Goldberg (citing Brodman), *The Executive Brain: Frontal Lobes and the Civilized Mind* (Oxford: Oxford University Press, 2001), page 33.

"Imagine a symphony orchestra": Thomas Brown, *Attention Deficit Disorder: The Unfocused Mind in Children and Adults* (New Haven, CT: Yale University Press, 2005).

It also affords us the necessary self-control: Russell Barkley, *Executive Functions* (New York: Guilford Press, 2002).

Take a look at this list of problems: Adapted from K. B. Powell and K. K. S. Voeller, "Prefrontal Executive Function Syndromes in Children," *Journal of Child Neurology* 19, no. 10 (October 2004).

The prefrontal cortex allows us to form: Brown, *Attention Deficit Disorder*; Goldberg, *The Executive Brain*; H. Gardner and S. Morgan, "Hill, Skill, and Will: Executive Function from a Multiple Intelligence Perspective," in L. Meltzer, editor, *Executive Function in Education* (New York: Guilford Press, 2007).

Working memory's job is not only to hold information: Goldberg, *The Executive Brain.*

Organization can be broken down into two categories: Mel Levine, *A Mind at a Time* (New York: Simon & Schuster, 2002).

"the organ of civilization": Goldberg, *The Executive Brain.*

"social animals": Barkley, *ADHD and the Nature of Self-Control.*

Hill, skill, and will: Gardner and Morgan, "Hill, Skill, and Will."

"Skill development predominates": Ibid., page 25.

"who do not limit themselves to climbing": Ibid., page 27.

"like a person needing a loan": Dr. Haim G. Ginott, *Between Parent and Teenager* (New York: Macmillan, 1967).

Zone of Proximal Development: Lev Vygotsky, *Mind in Society: The Development of Higher Psychological Processes* (Cambridge, MA: Harvard University Press, 1987).

Here are the steps to constructing a solid plan: Adapted from Mel Levine, *Educational Care* (Cambridge, MA: Educational Publishing Service, 2001).

Marydee Sklar, who developed the Sklar Process: Marydee Sklar, *Seeing My Time* (Portland, OR: Aguana Publishing, 2012).

Mantras: Mary Solanto, *Cognitive-Behavioral Therapy for Adult ADHD* (New York: Guilford Press, 2011).

Procrastination expert: Neil Fiore, *The Now Habit* (New York: Penguin, 1989), page 25.

Recently Canadian researchers: Shirley S. Wang, "To Stop Procrastinating, Start by Understanding the Emotions Involved," *Wall Street Journal*,

updated August 31, 2015, accessed September 28, 2015, www.wsj.com/
articles/to-stop-procrastinating-start-by-understanding-whats-really-
going-on-1441043167.

CHAPTER 5

"The cultivation of boys": David Von Drehle, "The Myth About Boys,"
Time magazine, July 26, 20007.
"not only feel the pressure to be masculine": Kindlon and Thompson, 2001.
it is other boys they look to: Michael Kimmel, *Manhood in America: A
Cultural History* (New York: Free Press, 1996).
Teenage boys form a boy credo: William Pollack, *Real Boys: Rescuing Our
Boys from the Myths of Boyhood* (New York: Henry Holt, 1998).
Boys will see them as feminine: Michael Kimmel, *Guyland: The Perilous
World Where Boys Become Men: Understanding the Critical Years
Between 16 and 26* (New York: HarperCollins, 2008).
The unspoken oath of boyhood: Ka'eo Vasconcellos, "What Maketh a
Man?" TEDxTalks, June 17, 2013, http://tedxtalks.ted.com/video/What-
Maketh-a-Man-Kaeo-Vasconce.
When academics write about masculinity: James R. Mahalik, Glenn Good,
and Matt Englar-Carlson, "Masculinity Scripts, Presenting Concerns
and Help Seeking: Implications for Practice and Training," *Professional
Psychology, Research and Practice* 34 no. 2 (2003): 123–31.
"Highs and lows": Jeffrey Marx, *Season of Life: A Football Star, a Boy,
a Journey to Manhood* (New York: Simon & Schuster, 2007), Kindle
edition, pages 11–12.
The sociologist Nancy Chodorow: Nancy Chodorow, *The Reproduction
of Mothering* (Berkeley: University of California Press,
1978).
"A son is a son till he gets a wife": Beth Dorogusker, "Sex Differences in
Psychological Separation," unpublished doctoral dissertation, 1989.
Forever jockeying for a position of power: Deborah Tannen, *You Just Don't
Understand!: Women and Men in Conversation* (New York: Harper,
1990), page 156.
For boys it's not who, but *what*, you know: Bruce Pirie, *Teenage Boys and
High School English* (Portsmouth, NH: Heinemann, 2002).
hang out around a specific activity: Kathryn Dindia and Mike Allen, "Sex
Differences in Self-Disclosure: A Meta-Analysis," *Psychological Bulletin*
112 (1992): 106–24; Leonard Sax, *Why Gender Matters* (New York:
Doubleday, 2005).
Deborah Tannen, a linguist who focuses on gender differences: Tannen, *You
Just Don't Understand!*
Generally, boys are able to form close friendships: Niobe Way, *Deep Secrets:*

Boys' Friendships and the Crisis of Connections (Cambridge, MA: Presidents and Fellows of Harvard University, 2011).

Today's hookup culture: Mahalik et al., "Masculinity Scripts, Presenting Concerns and Help Seeking."

the "mask of masculine bravado": Pollack, *Real Boys*, page 5.

Women, on the other hand, feel shame: Brené Brown, *Daring Greatly: How the Courage to Be Vulnerable Transforms the Way We Live, Love, Parent, and Lead* (New York: Avery, 2012). Brené Brown has taught us a lot about shame; also see "Listening to Shame" (TED talk, March 2012), https://www.ted.com/talks/brene_brown_listening_to_shame?language=en; "The Power of Vulnerability" (TED talk, June 2010), https://www.ted.com/talks/brene_brown_on_vulnerability.

Don't nag: Tannen, *You Just Don't Understand!*

"emotional schedules": Pollack, *Real Boys*.

Give him the "silent treatment": Alon Gratch, *If Men Could Talk: Translating the Secret Language of Men* (New York: Little Brown, 2001).

a story from nature told by Carl Safina: Carl Safina, "Tapping Your Inner Wolf," *New York Times* op-ed, June 6, 2015.

"We need to stop beating the softness out of boys": Vasconcellos, "What Maketh a Man?"

The payoff, according to Kindlon and Thomspson: Kindlon and Thompson, *Raising Cain*, page 89.

CHAPTER 6

Even at Punahou, where students: Chai Reddy, personal communication.

Ka'eo understands why the boys: Ka'eo Vasconcellos, personal communication.

Books such as *The War Against Boys*: Christina Hoff Sommers, *The War Against Boys: How Misguided Feminism Is Harming Young Men* (New York: Touchstone Books, 2002); Lenoard Sax, *Boys Adrift: The Five Factors Driving the Growing Epidemic of Unmotivated Boys and Underachieving Young Men* (New York: Touchstone Books, 2007); Peg Tyre, *The Trouble with Boys: A Surprising Report Card on Our Sons, Their Problems at School, and What Parents and Educators Must Do* (New York: Crown Publishing, 2008).

Richard Whitmire writes: Richard Whitmire, "Boy Trouble," *New Republic*, January 23, 2006.

According to the Department of Education: http://www.nationsreportcard.gov. Scores in math and reading are reported at three milestones, ages nine, thirteen, and seventeen (corresponding to grades four, eight, and twelve). Since 1971, although the overall gap between whites and blacks and whites and Hispanics has narrowed, with the exception of age nine for English and age seventeen for math, girls have consistently outpaced boys. Since 2008 these gains were lost, but thirteen-year-old boys caught up to girls in reading.

A recent analysis of nearly 370 studies: Daniel Voyer and Susan Voyer, "Gender Difference in Scholastic Achievement: A Meta-Analysis," *Psychological Bulletin,* April 28, 2014.

And this problem is worldwide: The Voyers' analysis covered thirty countries. According to a study conducted in 2002 by the Organization for Economic Cooperation (reported in Whitmire, "Boy Trouble"), a gender gap existed in nineteen out of twenty-seven countries studied. The gap was widest in Greece, Iceland, Italy, Portugal, and Spain.

Compared with boys, girls: Whitmire, "Boy Trouble"; Hoff Sommers, *The War Against Boys*; Michael Gurian and Kathy Stevens, *The Mind of Boys: Saving Our Boys from Falling Behind in School and in Life* (New York: Jossey-Bass, 2005); http://www.pewresearch.org/fact-tank/2014/03/06/womens-college-enrollment-gains-leave-men-behind.

In her book, she writes that: Hoff Sommers, *The War Against Boys*, page 75.

Worse, arguments justifying a boy crisis: C. Rivers and R. Barnett, "How the News Media Peddle Junk Science," *American Journalism Review,* December 2011–January 2012, accessed July 25, 2015, http://ajrarchive.org/Article.asp?id=5212; D. F. Halpern, L. Eliot, R. S. Bigler, R. A. Fabes, L. D. Hanish, J. Hyde, L. S. Liben, and C. L. Martin, "The Pseudoscience of Single-Sex Schooling," *Science: Education Forum* 333 (September 23, 2011), accessed July 25, 2015, http://science.sciencemag.org/content/333/6050/1706.

even the primary investigator yells "foul": Tyre, *The Trouble with Boys*, Kindle edition, page 177.

The truth is that boys' and girls' brains: Lise Eliot, *Pink Brain, Blue Brain: How Small Differences Grow into Troublesome Gaps—and What We Can Do About It* (New York: Houghton, Mifflin, Harcourt, 2009), page 5.

in one study, parents of newborn girls: M. Stern and K. H. Karraker, "Sex Stereotyping of Infants: A Review of Gender Labeling Studies," *Sex Roles* 20 (1989): 501–22 (as reported in Eliot, *Pink Brain, Blue Brain*).

Let's take a closer look: This discussion of cognitive gender differences is based on research summarized by Eliot, *Pink Brain, Blue Brain.*

However, boys' visual-spatial skills do develop ahead: Jillian Lauer, Hallie B. Udelson, Sung O. Jeon, and Stella F. Lourenco, "An Early Sex Difference in Relation Between Mental Rotation and Object Preference," *Frontiers in Psychology* 6, no. 558 (2015), frontiersin.org; Susan C. Levine, Janellen Huttenlocher, Amy Taylor, and Adela Langrock, (1999). "Early Sex Differences in Spatial Skill," *Developmental Psychology* 35, no. 4 (1999): 940–49.

"verbal ability is actually one of the smaller sex differences": Ibid., page 146.
"it is this difference": Ibid., page 140.
girl chimps are more attentive to their teachers: E. V. Lonsdorf, L. E. Eberly, and A. E. Pusey, "Sex Differences in Learning in Chimpanzees," *Nature* 428 (April 15, 2004): 715–16.
Dan Kindlon and Michael Thompson explain that: Kindlon and Thompson, *Raising Cain*, page 31.
Investigators Thomas DiPrete and Claudia Buchman: Thomas Diprete and Claudia Buchmann, "The Secret Behind College Completion: Girls, Boys, and the Power of Eighth Grade Grades," Third Way Next, 2014, http://content.thirdway.org/publications/813/NEXT - The_Secret_Behind_College_Completion.pdf.
Ka'eo feels that boys need lots of encouragement: Vasconcellos, personal communication.
Kindlon and Thompson clearly agree: Kindlon and Thompson, *Raising Cain*, page 38.
Daniel H. Pink, author of: Daniel H. Pink, *Drive: The Surprising Truth About What Motivates Us* (New York: Riverhead Press, 2009).
So when you study algebra: Steinberg, *The Age of Opportunity*, page 36.
Here is what he had to say: Reddy, personal communication.
David Murray, a high school math teacher: David Murray, personal communication.
Bruce Pirie, a high school English teacher: Bruce Pirie, *Teenage Boys and High School English* (Portsmouth, NH: Heinemann Press, 2002).
Richard Louv, author of: Richard Louv, *Last Child in the Woods* (Chapel Hill, NC: Algonquin Books, 2005).
Dr. Leonard Sax: Sax, *"Boys Adrift."*
One study showed: Gilbert, Susan, *A Field Guide to Boys and Girls* (New York: Harper Collins, 2000).

PART II
According to researchers Deci and Ryan: Edward L. Deci and Richard M. Ryan, "The 'What' and 'Why' of Goal Pursuits: Human Needs and the Self-Determination of Behavior," *Psychological Inquiry* 11, no. 4 (2000): 227–68.

CHAPTER 8
Researchers Edward Deci and Richard Ryan: E. L. Deci and R. M. Ryan, *Intrinsic Motivation and Self-Determination in Human Behavior* (New York: Plenum, 1985).
He finds video games inherently interesting: C. P. Niemiec and R. M. Ryan, "Autonomy, Competence, and Relatedness in the Classroom: Applying

Self-Determination Theory to Educational Practice," *Theory and Research in Education* (2009), Sage Publications.

as Laurence Steinberg points out: Steinberg, *The Age of Opportunity.*

Years ago, the psychologist Walter Mischel: W. Mischel, Y. Shoda, and P. Peake, "The Nature of Adolescent Competencies Predicted by Preschool Delay of Gratification," *Journal of Personality and Social Psychology* 54, no. 4 (1988): 687–96.

Rewards and punishments might offer a short-term solution: Mireille Joussemet, René Landry, and Richard Koestner, "A Self-Determination Theory Perspective on Parenting," *Canadian Psychology* 49, no. 3 (2008): 194–200.

a discovery of Sigmund Freud's: Sigmund Freud, "The Economic Problem of Masochism," in J. Strachey, editor, *The Standard Edition of the Complete Works of Sigmund Freud*, volume 19 (London: Hogarth Press, 1924), pages 155–70.

According to psychologist Wendy Grolnick: W. S. Grolnick, *The Psychology of Parental Control: How Well-Meant Parenting Backfires* (New York and London: Psychology Press, 2003), page 53.

internalization is the process of turning: W. S. Grolnick, E. Deci, H. Eghari, B. Patrick, and D. Leone, "Facilitating Internalization: The Self-Determination Theory Perspective," *Journal of Personality* 62 (March 1994).

This developmental process happens in a series of stages: Adapted from R. M. Ryan and J. P. Connell, "Perceived Locus of Causality and Internalization: Examining Reasons for Acting in Two Domains," *Journal of Personality and Social Psychology* 57 (1989): 749–61; W. S. Grolnick, E. Deci, H. Eghari, B. Patrick, and D. Leone, "Facilitating Internalization: The Self-Determination Theory Perspective," *Journal of Personality* 62 (March 1994); M. Vansteenkiste, E. Sierens, B. Soenens, K. Luyckjx, and W. Lens, "The Quality of Motivation Matters," *Journal of Educational Psychology* 101, no. 3 (2009): 671–88.

CHAPTER 9

being able to manage the anxiety and self-doubt: M. J. Zimmer-Gembeck and W. A. Collins, "Autonomy Development During Adolescence," in G. R. Adams and M. Berzonsky, editors, *Blackwell Handbook of Adolescence* (Oxford: Blackwell Publishers, 2003), pages 175–204.

The optimal environment for motivaiton to grow: Grolnick, *The Psychology of Parental Control.*

This support becomes vital: Zimmer-Gembeck and Collins, "Autonomy Development During Adolescence"; J. Allen, S. Hauser, C. Eickholt,

K. Bell, and T. O'Connor, "Autonomy and Relatedness in Family
Interactions as Predictors of Expressions of Negative Adolescent
Affect," *Journal of Research on Adolescence* 4 (1994): 535–52; C. J.
Adams, "NAEP Study Finds Jump in Students Taking Tough Courses,"
Education Week, April 13, 2011, accessed September 20, 2015, http://
www.edweek.org/ew/articles/2011/04/13/28naep.h30.html.

Any transition to adulthood: L. Steinberg and S. Silverberg, "The
Vicissitudes of Autonomy in Early Adolescence," *Child Development* 57
(1986): 841–51.

Dr. Wendy Grolnick, a leading expert: Grolnick, *The Psychology of Parental
Control*, page 53.

Other researchers concur: J. S. Eccles, D. Early, K. Fraser, E. Belansky, and
K. McCarthy, "The Relation of Connection, Regulation, and Support
for Autonomy to Adolescents' Functioning," *Journal of Adolescent
Research* 12, no. 2 (1997): 263–86; K. M. Best, S. T. Hauser, and J.
Allen, "Predicting Young Adult Competencies: Adolescent Era Parent
and Individual Differences," *Journal of Adolescent Reserach* 12 (1997):
90–112; S. Dornbusch, P. Ritter, H. Leiderman, and D. Roberts, "The
Relation of Parenting Style to Adolescent School Performance," *Child
Development* 58, no. 5 (1987): 1244–57; L. Steinberg, S. Lamborn,
S. Dornbusch, and N. Darling, "Impact of Parenting Practices on
Adolescent Achievement: Authoritative Parenting, School Involvement,
and Encouragement to Succeed," *Child Development* 63 (1992):
1266–81.

Houston Dougharty of Grinnell College: T. Gabriel, "Students, Welcome to
College. Parents, Go Home," *New York Times*, August 22, 2010.

when parents—in Madeline Levine's words: M. Levine, *The Price of
Privilege* (New York: HarperCollins, 2006).

One of Deci and Ryan's most surprising findings: E. L. Deci and R. M.
Ryan, "The 'What' and 'Why' of Goal Pursuits: Human Needs and the
Self-Determination of Behavior," *Psychological Inquiry* 11, no. 4 (2000):
277–68.

Others have found that rewards: As reported in ibid.

CHAPTER 10

my favorite parenting writer, Dr. Haim G. Ginott: Ginott, *Between Parent
and Teenager.*

You cannot be the "defender of change": W. R. Miller and S. Rollnick,
Motivational Interviewing: Preparing People for Change, 2nd edition
(New York: Guilford Press, 2002).

Be an advocate, not a prosecutor: Ginott, *Between Parent and Teenager.*

List of Strengths: Miller and Rollnick, *Motivational Interviewing*.

"Understanding is love's other name": T. N. Hanh, *How to Love* (Berkeley, CA: Parallax Press, 2015).

When you see this kind of resistance: S. Naar-King and M. Suarez, *Motivational Interviewing with Adolescents and Young Adults* (New York: Guilford Press, 2011).

follow the acronym EAR: Miller and Rollnick, *Motivational Interviewing*.

"Remember when I asked you to rate": Ibid.

Common Ways Teens Trap Parents and How to Avoid Them: Wolf, *Get Out of My Life*.

give some advance thought to where: R. Greene, *The Explosive Child: A New Approach for Understanding and Parenting Easily Frustrated, Chronically Inflexible Children* (New York: HarperCollins, 1998).

As Anthoy Wolf has wisely observed: Wolf, *Get Out of My Life*.

CHAPTER 11

Self-awareness is the only way: Brown, *Daring Greatly*.

Psychoanalysts have written about: Alice Miller, *The Drama of the Gifted Child* (New York: Basic Books, 1997); D. W. Winnicott, *Maturational Processes and the Facilitating Environment: Studies in the Theory of Emotional Development* (New York: International University Press, 1965).

Like Miss Havisham's room: Charles Dickens, *Great Expectations* (London: Chapman & Hall, 1861).

And in the words of the poet Kahlil Gibran: Kahlil Gibran, *The Prophet* (New York: Alfred A. Knopf, 1923).

CHAPTER 12

"Experience . . . is merely the name": Oscar Wilde, *The Picture of Dorian Grey* (New York: Dover Thrift Editions, 1993).

It's *The Little Engine That Could*: W. Piper, *The Little Engine That Could* (New York: Platt & Munk, 1930).

Psychologists have been studying it: A. Bandura, *Self-Efficacy: The Exercise of Control* (New York: Freeman, 1997); D. E. Schunk and D. S. Miller, "Self-Efficacy and Adolescents' Motivation," in F. Pajares and T. Urdan, *Academic Motivation of Adolescents* (Greenwich, CT: Information Age Publishing, 2002), pages 29–52.

Carol Dweck, one of the top: C. Dweck, *Mindset: The New Psychology of Success* (New York: Ballantine Books, 2006).

By comparison, the kids with a growth mind-set: L. S. Blackwell, K. H. Trzeniewski, and C. S. Dweck, "Implicit Theories of Intelligence Predict Acheivement Across an Adolescent Transition: A Longitudinal Study and an Intervention," *Child Development* 78, no. 1 (2007): 246–63.

Dweck concluded that: Dweck, *Mind-Set*, Kindle edition, page 57.

To help your son do the same: Dweck, *Mind-Set*.

And he's not alone: M. Brown, "How Driving a Taxi Changes London Cabbies' Brains," *Wired Science*, December 9, 2011, accessed September 1, 2015, http://www.wired.com/2011/12/london-taxi-driver-memory.

Two neuropsychologists at University College London: K. Woolett and E. A. Maguire, "Acquiring 'the Knowledge' of London's Layout Drives Structural Brain Changes," *21* (2011), 2019–14.

When your son does well: M. L. Kamis and C. S. Dweck, "Person Versus Process Praise and Criticism: Implications for Contingent Self-Worth and Coping," *Developmental Psychology* 35 (1999): 835–47; E. A. Pomerantz, W. S. Grolnick, and E. C. Price, "The Role of Parents in How Children Approach Acheivement," in A. J. Elliot and C. S. Dweck, *Handbook of Competence and Motivation* (New York: Guilford Press, 2005), pages 259–78.

When children feel that a parent's love: Grolnick, *The Psychology of Parental Control*.

CHAPTER 13

One of my favorite quotes about parenting: Wolf, *Get Out of My Life*, page 7.

Several years ago, writer Jennifer Senior: J. Senior, "All Joy, No Fun," *New York* magazine, July 4, 2010.

The Dalai Lama said: A. W. Schaef, *Meditations for Living in Balance: Daily Soulutions for People Who Do Too Much* (New York: HarperCollins, 2000).

In the words of *Washington Post* columnist Michael Gerson: M. Gerson, "Saying Goodbye to My Child, the Youngster," *Washington Post*, August 19, 2013.

The joy your son achieves: This conception of happiness comes from Greek philosophers such as Aristotle and Plato, who felt that that *eudaimonia* (the word most often translated "happiness") is *kinesis* ("activity") in accordance with one's high *estareté* (often translated "excellence"). According to Dr. Naomi Reshotko, professor of philosophy at the University of Denver, "even lazy people want to be eudaimonic" (personal communication).

Acknowledgments

Words can only approximate the deep gratitude I feel to so many who have touched this project—some by reading every word and others by offering gestures of support both large and small. Some I have known for decades, and others I was fortunate to meet as a result of this book.

First, I would like to thank my wonderful team of editors at Sterling Publishing: Jennifer Williams, Renee Yewdaev, and Laura Jorstad. Jennifer initially championed the project, then guided it deftly with her kind but steady hand. Her enthusiasm and reassurance made light work of what could be an arduous project. Renee and Laura approached the manuscript with precision, bringing clarity while being ever mindful of my voice as an author. I'd also like to thank the other team members at Sterling who have helped bring this book together: Marilyn Kretzer, Lorie Pagnozzi, Elizabeth Lindy, Blanca Oliviery, Ardi Alspach, and Ellen Hudson.

I am also grateful to three highly skilled and brilliant writer/editors. Savannah Ashour was instrumental, Catherine Crawford ensured that my writing was crisp and lucid, and Peg Rosen, a seasoned journalist, challenged me, as only she can, to think more clearly. I would also like to thank Gale Alexander, who keeps me not only focused and organized, but also lightens my mood every day.

My colleagues Sylvia Pollock and Joel Morgan added depth and wisdom to this book. Sylvia is one of those who generously read every word, and Joel helped out immensely, reading Chapter 3. I would also like to thank Clare Cosentino, Jeremy Leeds, Dan Rothstein, Ann Hicks, Carla Massey, Karen Wieland of the South Orange Maplewood Parenting Center, Peter Lewis of the Winston School, and the Montclair Child Study Team for offering me the chance to present my ideas to parents and professionals.

Jane Folger, Irene Langlois, and Robin Whalen, librarians at the Maplewood Public Library have been extremely helpful.

I have had so many wonderful teachers and guides. Karen Bloom and Ann LaRocque first taught me about adolescents when I was barely a teenager myself, Dr. Salvador Minuchin believed in me early on as a writer and therapist, and Dr. Rafael Javier taught me, well, everything.

I have been deeply inspired and moved by the patients whose stories and struggles are reflected on every page of this book. It has been a privilege to be entrusted with their confidence and a pleasure to be enlivened by their spirit. I am equally indebted to those who graciously answered my questions and offered insights of their own: Chai Reddy, Ka'eo Vasconcellos, Mary Solanto, Mark Kelly, John Turvey, Noah Hirshman, and David Murray.

I am blessed with many wonderful friends, whose enthusiasm and excitement is deeply appreciated: Jane Ostacher and Jim Poderhetz, Laurie Berkman and David Trager, Pam and Evan Bard, David and Lauren Meisels, Leslie Reingold and Tom Clavin, Michele Sacks and Alon Gratch, Michael Fayne, and Bob Krasner. I am especially grateful to Jim, a filmmaker, and Tom, a writer, who shared with me their wisdom about the creative process. Bob graciously lent his artistic gifts and photographic skill. Alon, an accomplished author and psychologist, dedicated countless hours to discuss this material and provide a sounding board.

And then there are those without whose help this book would truly never have been written. Cathy Hemming, my lifelong friend and agent provided encouragement, expertise, insight, and patience. This book could not have been written without her, and I am a better person for having known her. My parents Donald and Roslyn Price nurtured in me a love of psychology and writing. I only wish my father could have lived to see this book become a reality. My brother Eric, and his husband Carl Bazil provided steady support and sage advice. My in-laws Ben and Claire Dorogusker were always on hand for a welcomed boost, as was my sister-in law Nina Greenberg. My nieces Lauren and Nicolette Greenberg offered an enthusiastic cheering section, but also provided their own insights into the adolescent male.

My children, Jonah and Sam, have been a continual source of pride and contentment. They provided insight, support, and the welcomed distraction of humor. Each challenged me to think more rigorously and more openly. They taught me so much and have truly been my well of motivation.

And finally, I am deeply indebted to my wife Beth. She has been my muse, inspiration, and prefrontal cortex. She nurtured my desire to write a book from the very beginning, offered sound guidance throughout the process, and graciously sacrificed countless weekends to the process. Most important, she always knew I could.

About the Author

Dr. Adam Price, a clinical psychologist and author, has worked with children, adolescents, and their families for more than twenty-five years. He is an expert in learning disabilities and Attention Deficit Hyperactive Disorder. He has supervised and trained numerous clinicians in family and child therapy. Dr. Price has written for both academic and popular publications, including *The Wall Street Journal* and *Family Circle Magazine,* and currently writes a column for *Psychology Today.* He has presented nationally to parents and educators and has appeared frequently on television and radio to discuss topics ranging from child discipline to the impact of video games on children. Dr. Price maintains a private practice in New York City and in Chatham, New Jersey. He and his wife have raised two teenagers. For more information, please visit dradamprice.com

Index